SALLEYLAND

SALLEYLAND

WILDLIFE ADVENTURES *in* SWAMPS, SANDHILLS, *and* FORESTS

WHIT GIBBONS

THE UNIVERSITY OF ALABAMA PRESS

Tuscaloosa

The University of Alabama Press
Tuscaloosa, Alabama 35487-0380
uapress.ua.edu

Inquiries about reproducing material from this work should
be addressed to the University of Alabama Press.

Typeface: Adobe Caslon Pro

Cover image: Courtesy of Whit Gibbons
Cover design: Lori Lynch

Cataloging-in-Publication data is available from the Library of Congress.
ISBN: 978-0-8173-6064-1
E-ISBN: 978-0-8173-9426-4

To Carolyn Gibbons, with appreciation for her
unwavering support of my involvement with Salleyland
and other environmental projects

I find solace, inspiration, and exhilaration in nature. Issues there are boiled down to the simplest imperative: survive. Sometimes my existence seems to hang in the balance of challenges professional and personal, external and internal. What allows me to survive day to day is having nature as my guide.

J. DREW LANHAM, *The Home Place: Memoirs of a Colored Man's Love Affair with Nature*

Study nature, love nature, stay close to nature. It will never fail you.

FRANK LLOYD WRIGHT

Contents

Acknowledgments

WHEN I WROTE SCIENTIFIC BOOKS AND JOURNAL ARTICLES, MY AC-knowledgment sections were often longer than most editors wanted to edit and publishers wanted to publish. But I never accomplished any of the research without the help of many mentors, students and other colleagues, friends, and family. I like to credit them all for dealing with me in constructive ways. Likewise, the Salleyland project has been carried on the shoulders of hundreds of visitors. I appreciate their participation in field trips and in discussions on the back porch or on the land itself.

First, I appreciate the family members who have spent from a few to dozens of days at Salleyland: Ron Curtis, Bill Fitts, Allison Gibbons, Anne Gibbons, Carolyn Gibbons, Jennifer Gibbons, Laura Gibbons, Michael Gibbons, Parker Gibbons, Jacob Harris, Justin Harris, Keith Harris, Nick Harris, Susan Lane Harris, Jamie Hebden, Beth Heckman, Ron Heckman, James High, Jennifer High, Jim High, Sam High, Austin Levin, Ed Passerini, JoLee Passerini, Tyler Perry, Connie Rasmussen, Eyvin Rasmussen, Anita Smith, and Wayne Smith.

Many people have contributed to environmental education at Salleyland by finding and identifying flora and fauna, facilitating visits by experts, and making habitat modifications that have enhanced the Salleyland experience. They include Robert Abernethy, John Alexander, Kimberly Andrews, Jim Angley, Chad Argabright, Kimi Artita, Huck Bagby, Laura Bagwell, Phillip Baker, Jim Beasley, Matthew Beasley, Michael Beasley, Rochelle Beasley, Christopher Benavides, Zachariah Benjamin, Claire Bennett, Dylan Bennett, Jeff Bennett, Kathleen Bennett, Molly Bennett, Patrick Bennett, Steve Bennett, Emily Bertucci, Lenny Birch, Emily Bonilla, Greg Boozer, Kylie Bosch, Nick Bossenbroek, April Bowen, Bradley Bowen, Joshua Bowen, Bri Bowerman, Kathy Boyle, Jimmy Boyleston, John Brecht, Jerry Bright, Kyle Brown, Emma Browning, Kurt Buhlmann, Gary Burger,

Heidi Burke, Vince Burke, Jackie Holmes Burns, Danty Busbee, Nita Busbee, Walter Busbee, John Byrd, Grant Cagle, Mark Cagle, Nicolette Cagle, Parham Cain, Karen Cajz, Craig Callender, Elliot Callender, Liam Callender, Lois Callender, Demetrius Calloway, Jeff Camper, Jan Ciegler, Zane Clardy, Mike Collins, Justin Congdon, Nancy Congdon, Jonathan Cooley, Preston Cooper, Wyles Cornwell, Emily Curry, Tate Curry, Brett DeGregorio, John Demko, Joe Deskevich, Michelle Dillman, Will Dillman, Wes Dixon, Mike Dorcas, Zack Dorcas, Mary Douglass, Aaron Dowdy, Billy Dukes, Brandon Eargle, David Eargle, Julia Eargle, Nicholas Edge, Jeff Edgemon, Thomas Ervin, David Eslinger, Lynn Faust, Pat Ferral, Hilda Flamholtz, Dick Flood (a.k.a. Okenfenokee Joe), Rick Flood, Marolyn Floyd, Rooney Floyd, Kate Flynn, Nicole Haigh Flynn, Tim Flynn, Wesley Flynn, Allen Fornwald, Bob Franklin, Michael Brandon Frazier, Mike Frees, Bill Gandrud Gardner, Hanna Gerke, Julia Geschke, John Gillespie, Sha'nia Latia Glenn, Dre'Shawn Jonte Goode-Legette, Sean Graham, Judy Greene, Kathryn Greene, Stuart Greeter, Blake Gregory, Karen Gregory, Logan Gregory, Matthew Gregory, Andrew Grosse, Kylie Elizabeth Hackett, Cris Hagen, Matt Hamilton, Bob Hamlin, Marsha Hamlin, Phil Harpootlian, Bess Harris, Kate Hartley, David Lee Haskins, Natalie Haydt, Tyrone Hayes, Tevin Hayward, Jim Hefner, George Heinrich, John Hewlett, Wally Holland, Jeff Holmes, Joey Holmes, David Hothem, Meg Hoyle, Martinais Hudson, Cameron Huston, Ellen Huston, Rick Huston, Sylvia Huston, Paul Jackson, Melissa Jamison, John Jensen, Daryll Johnson, Emma Johnson, Georgia Claire Johnson, Mandy Johnson, Amanda Jones, Morris Jones, Tom Jones, Kelly Joyner, Paul Kalbach, Wade Kalinowsky, Dave Kastner, Marty Kastner, Robert Kennamer, Josh Key, Taylor Lindsey Kinter, Bellamy Klein, Elizabeth Klein, Richard Klein, Laura Kojima, Bret Ladrie, Amanda Lafferty, Stacey Lance, Anna Layton, Jonathan Layton, Eddie Lee, Linda Lee, Justin Lewandowski, Rob Lewis, Julian Lockwood, Stephanie Lockwood, Jeff Lovich, Sharon Lovich, Tom Luhring, Avery Luhring-Smith, Cole Luttrell, Andrew Lydeard, Matthew MacDonald, Michelle MacMillan, Patrick MacMillan, Kathryn Madden, Rudy Mancke, Mike Martin, J. Vaun McArthur, Eli McEuen, Luke McEuen, Phillip McEuen, Pearson McGovern, Ken McLeod, Kim McManus, Alan Merritt, Sharon Merritt, Troy Messick, Gary Mills, Mark Mills, Mark S. Mills, Tony Mills, Victoria Millsap, Joe Mitchell, Dwight Moffit, Tess Moody, Chris Moore, Chris Murphy, Gordon Murphy, John Nelson, Kerry Nelson, Jennifer Noel, Josh Noel, Nathan Noel, Dylan O'Hearn, Joy O'Keefe,

Emma Rose Parker, Joe Pechmann, Dan Peeples, Nakea Pennant, Dennis Perea, Pacifico Perea, Phillip Perea, Tricia Perea, La' Portia Perkins, Scott Pfaff, Todd Pierson, Melissa Pilgrim, Connor Pogue, Alena Poltorak, Stephen Prior, Renee Provost, Billy Quarles, Dan Quinn, Katie Rainwater, Talon Rainwater, Thomas Rainwater, Lannette Rangel, Collin Richter, Carter Ricks, Abby Riggs, Greg Ross, Hannah Royal, Chance Ruder, J. Clint Sawyer, Tristan Schramer, Dave Schuetrum, Philip Schulte, Anna Marie Scoccimaro, Mike Sears, Ray Semlitsch, Rebecca Sharitz, Harry Shealy, Marcus Sizemore, Philoma Skipper, Hank Smalling, Jennifer Smith, Juliana Smith, Michael Shelby Smith, Daniel Sollenberger, Chris Somers, Andrew Parton Sorrell, Vaughn Spearman, Peter Stangel, Ben Stegenga, Libby Sternhagen, Erica Summer Storey, Halle Denise Stump, Tony Taylor, Eli Teague, Putter Tiatragul, Brandon Tindall, Nick Tindall, Brian Todd, Logan Todd, Chuck Travis, Tracey Tuberville, Fredericka Tucker, Ben Turner, Margo Turner, Annalee Tutterow, Jonah Unger, Shannon Unger, Shem Unger, Phil Vogrinc, Mark Vukovich, Tyler Walters, Jennifer Wead, Margaret Wead, Richard Wead, Patricia West, Kristina Wheeler, John Williams, Ronald Craig Williamson III, Karen Willoughby, Ralph Willoughby, Robin Willoughby, J. D. Willson, Samantha Jane Winfree, Megan Winzeler, Jim Wood, Mary Olive Wood, Leslie Wright, Steve Wright, Sharon Yomtob, Billy Ray Young, Luke Young, Jake Zadik, Joe Zhou, Julie Ziemba, and Rita Zollinger.

The following people arranged for undergraduate herpetology classes or graduate students to sample in the study area: Jim Beasley (University of Georgia), Kurt Buhlmann and Tracey Tuberville (Savannah River Ecology Laboratory), Nicolette Cagle (Duke University), Mike Dorcas (Davidson College), Joe Pechmann (Western Carolina University), Melissa Pilgrim (University of South Carolina Upstate), and John Williams (South Carolina State University). Special thanks to Steve Bennett, John Byrd, Mike Gibbons, Parker Gibbons, Keith Harris, Nick Harris, and Sam High for extended individual efforts of many sorts.

For their helpful comments on selected sections, I thank Jim Beasley, Steve Bennett, John Byrd, Nicolette Cagle, Will Dillman, Mike Dorcas, Rooney Floyd, Andrew Grosse, John Jensen, Bobby Kennamer, Andrew Lydeard, Pearson McGovern, Tess Moody, Chris Moore, Scott Pfaff, Steve Platt, Bill Resetarits, and Peter Stangel.

I appreciate input from Ron Brenneman and Susan Lane Harris, both of whom read early drafts of this book. Special thanks go to Eli Greenbaum, who greatly improved the manuscript in its final form through suggestions, corrections, and thoughtful queries. I also thank Anne R. Gibbons for final editing and Claire Lewis Evans at the University of Alabama Press for navigating the manuscript through the publication process during the COVID-19 pandemic.

SALLEYLAND

Parker (*left*), Sam, and Nick fish from the Salleyland
bridge (2013). Photo by Jennifer G. High.

What Does a Retired Herpetologist Do?

I knew I had picked the right field assistant for the project when Parker scampered 20 feet up the sweetgum tree to capture a rough green snake while I held the flashlight on it from the stream below. His exhilaration at capturing the first green snake he had ever seen in the wild was evident by his ear-to-ear grin as he climbed down and got back in the canoe. My excitement was increased because this was the 14th herp (the accepted name for any reptile or amphibian) species added to our inventory of herpetofauna at our study site. Equally pleasing to me was the fact that Parker was only 10 years old, a promising sign of many wildlife adventures yet to come.

WHIT GIBBONS, "A PILOT HERPETOFAUNAL INVENTORY
ON PRIVATE LAND: IF KIDS CAN DO IT, ANYONE CAN"

THIS BOOK DOES NOT COME CLOSE TO BEING A MEMOIR, NOR IS IT INtended to be. I do write about personal issues, including the challenge of finding meaning in retirement. I consider aspects of purchasing and managing land as a personal conservation initiative. But primarily I celebrate the joy so many of us feel when we are outdoors and acknowledge the gratification of sharing discoveries with our companions. The setting for this book is South Carolina at a place called Salleyland. The same story of outdoor excursions could be told anywhere from Augusta, Maine, to Zephyrhills, Florida, from Anchorage, Alaska, to Zzyzx, California.

A bit of background seems appropriate at this point. I'll start with a roll call of immediate family members. Some are mentioned many times in this book, and explaining who's who every time would get tiresome. Carolyn and I were married in January 1963 and have four children: Laura, Jennifer

Anne, Susan Lane, and Mike. Mike and his wife (not sister), Jennifer, are parents of our only granddaughter, Allison, and our eldest grandson, Parker. Sam is the son of Jennifer Anne and her husband, Jim High. Our youngest grandchild, Nick, is the son of Susan Lane and Keith Harris. Laura and her husband, Ron, are the quintessential doting aunt and uncle.

Parker, Sam, and Nick have been the most frequent participants in critter searches and habitat explorations over the years. The three of them were featured in an article in the March/April 2019 issue of *Wildlife Professional* titled "A Pilot Herpetofaunal Study on Private Land: If Kids Can Do It, Anyone Can." Allison appears in several cameo roles. She was my primary family helper in constructing the swamp jumper boardwalk that made many of our field trips possible. She has become adept at using a chainsaw to remove trees and limbs that fall constantly across our stream.

When I first decided to retire, I had had a long career (forty-one years) as a University of Georgia professor involved in ecological research at the Savannah River Ecology Laboratory (SREL) in Aiken, South Carolina. I

The wildlife cabin, completed in 2012, overlooks a creek with a high biodiversity of fishes and invertebrates. Photo by author.

had conducted research projects at SREL and elsewhere; taught intermittently at the main university campus in Athens, Georgia; advised graduate students and undergraduate research interns; and avoided as many administrative responsibilities as possible.

For some career professionals retirement means continuing to do what you have always done. It was, after all, your career, and you got your life credentials and professional identity by excelling, or at least persisting, at it. I know retired biologists my age (and not unlike me in other ways) who go to the lab every day. They continue to conduct research, write scientific papers, and offer guidance to any student or faculty member who cares to listen. Many of my former colleagues are dead, not because they kept working too long but because we all get old and die. Many are still alive. I sometimes muse about outlasting them all and becoming the oldest living herpetologist in the world, which is probably at least a subliminal goal for most of us.

The impetus to retire from a tenured position at a university can come from various directions. My epiphany came when Tracey Tuberville, a young graduate student, came into the herpetology lab with two eastern mud turtles she had caught at one of our field sites. Over my research career, I had caught and marked thousands of individual turtles so I could follow growth and movement patterns. I had first marked both these turtles before Tracey was born! We had already documented in scientific publications that some turtles can live a long time. These two were several years older than their captor. Tracey was the first of my last cohort of graduate students, eight total, and as each began their residence at SREL, they worked in the local wetlands and eventually all caught turtles I had marked before they were born. I mentioned this to Mike, who said, "Dad, some of them are probably catching turtles you marked before their parents were born." I decided it was time to look into the possibility of retirement.

Most universities allow retirees to continue supervising their graduate students but not to take on new ones. Graduate students, at least the smart ones, act like they care what their major professor has to say. Such homage need not be paid to a retiree. Students who think they can learn from their elders seem to be on the wane, but maybe this has always been the way of the world. I think Socrates mentioned something of this nature around 400 BCE. Some academic ecologists stay on the job after retirement, not caring what those around them think. Many universities allow a bit of double-dipping by paying retirees to teach part-time or participate in someone else's research project. Some retirees have government grants still in play that can support them for months or years. I took advantage of such opportunities for a few years after officially retiring but eventually decided that I needed to really retire and take up a hobby.

To some people, retirement means receiving a superannuation pension and doing nothing that resembles their previous employment. My journey began with choices people face with retirement itself. To many, retirement means having the opportunity to engage in hobbies they always enjoyed but never had time for because a paying job kept interrupting them. Some career professionals have reservations about retiring because they have more work to accomplish in order to leave a lasting mark on their field.

I looked around to see what former colleagues, friends, and acquaintances had taken on as retirement activities—golf, woodworking, classic car restoration, gardening, boating, hunting, and fishing were but a few choices.

I am not a natural golfer. The only time I have been even a fairly good golfer (never a great one) was in college at the University of Alabama when my friend Butch Denman played alongside me and told me which club to use and how to hit the ball with it. Butch doesn't follow me around anymore, so spending my money on golf was out of the question.

I haven't the patience for woodworking nor the inclination to garden. My childhood knowledge of what's under the hood of automobiles was so limited it precluded my buying and restoring old muscle cars. My automotive expertise allows me to distinguish a green car from a red one and a '57 Chevy Bel Air from a Corvette.

I spent my career riding in boats on rivers, in the ocean, through swamps, and occasionally up onto logs, sand bars, and the shore itself. These boats and motors always belonged to someone else (usually a university or the federal government) and I had no emotional attachment to them. I had done enough boating.

As for fishing, I once published a scientific paper in the journal *Nature* based on a sample of twelve thousand largemouth bass and have probably caught more fish on rod and reel than most of those guys you see on the TV sports channels. But let me be the first to say, I am not an accomplished angler and get exceedingly annoyed with tangled lines, snagged hooks, and unruly bait. If I never do more than watch the grandkids fishing, I will be fine. Likewise, for hunting. I hunted squirrels and rabbits as a kid, killed more birds than I should have, but really only enjoyed the "getting out in the woods" aspect, not the shooting itself.

Allison teaches Nick how to shoot a bow and arrow. Initial plans
included a place near the cabin for outdoor recreational activities
such as horseshoes and archery. Photo by Mike Gibbons.

In short, I was not interested in pursuing any of those traditional retirement hobbies. So, what to do with my spare time? I heard from other
retirees that I would soon be consumed with small commitments here and
there and be "busier than ever." That, I knew, would not be true. (When a
retiree boasts of being busier than ever, I wonder how hard they worked at
their paying job.)

Carolyn and I came up with the idea of buying a few acres of land. I had
spent my career pursuing my passion, which was to spend a lot of time outdoors. Why not spend my retirement engaged in an activity I already knew I
liked and would never get tired of? We had owned some land when our children were younger but had sold that property long ago during the one year
when all four of them were in college. I decided a small tract of worthless
farmland with poor soil and little to offer any self-respecting farmer would
be a good investment for my purpose: to have a wooded retreat I could enjoy
whenever the mood struck. Spending time there with my grandkids was a

gratifying prospect. The three grandsons, ages one to four, and Allison, who was eight, all lived within an hour's drive.

Many real estate agents in the county we live in make a fine living selling houses to retirees from other parts of the country. Furthermore, the recreational horse industry—racehorse training for the Kentucky Derby, dressage, polo, traditional fox hunts with real hounds—thrives in Aiken and the surrounding area. The winter people, who arrive in autumn and leave in spring, include wealthy horse owners and their entourage of jockeys, trainers, and stable hands. Expensive horses require the finest equestrian facilities. Much of the rural property in the county is deemed "equestrian land," which can be transformed into whatever a horse lover might need. Equestrian land is expensive because horse owners who require a large tract can afford the purchase and upkeep. Demand exceeds supply.

I set out on my search for suitable land with an excellent Realtor (Ron Pope). Ron and I looked at several tracts already cleared of most trees to provide areas suitable for development into ideal grazing pastures for horses or for building upscale stables. Some places had plenty of trees and even an occasional lake or stream, ideal for horseback riding and accordingly out of my price range. The farther we got from town and its pervasive equestrian mentality, the cheaper the land got. One day, Ron asked if I would like to look at a piece of property in an adjacent county. The land lay between two sleepy southern towns so small that neither had a grocery store. Property values on that side of the county line dropped as much as 50 percent.

After the usual hassles and exasperations of buying property anywhere, Carolyn and I owned thirty-five acres of worthless swampland and second-, third-, or fourth-growth hardwood forest. We purchased those thirty-five acres for what we would have paid for about six acres in the upmarket countryside where I had been looking. Same price with lots more room and only twenty-five miles from home. In my spare time, which would be considerable, I could walk around the land looking for reptiles, amphibians, and other wildlife—as I had done for my entire career, indeed my entire life. I could be there in forty minutes, even during rush hour, which doesn't really exist in rural South Carolina.

Private land has many environmental stories to tell and can entertain forever. My focus at Salleyland has been to enjoy and write about the habitats and associated wildlife with an emphasis on what I have learned on my own and from others about the actors on the revolving stage of the natural world. I extol the value of private property, from backyards to larger protected tracts, as environmental sanctuaries for native wildlife. Parks—city, state, or federal—can also serve as outdoor laboratories for uncovering nature's myriad mysteries for personal gratification.

In acquiring private land, the responsibilities of landownership—deed preparations, taxes, road access—must be dealt with. Then a basic behavioral trait rises to the surface: territoriality. Trespassers, especially hunters of deer and turkey, led me to identify boundaries, post No Trespassing signs, and set up fences, in the spirit of Robert Frost. Wariness toward uninvited humans became normal behavior. Building a cabin further staked our claim amid the natural inhabitants of plants and animals. Clearing out some vegetation,

The family enjoys boating, swimming, and rope swinging in the creek that runs alongside the cabin. Photo by Mike Gibbons.

building picnic tables and a firepit, establishing paths, and hanging a rope swing over the creek soon followed. I looked forward to meeting our wildlife neighbors. Duck boxes, bird feeders, bat boxes, and trellises were welcome mats, but I knew I was the one who was the visitor, in their home. I needed a long-term plan.

Make a Plan

It was raining when I left, but I had to get out for a snapping turtle in the middle of SNAP Road, the first one we have found! It seemed small to be a gravid female but had clearly scraped out dirt, presumably for a nest, although the soil in the tire rut was too hard. I never dreamed we would find so many kinds of reptiles and amphibians. All the other animals and plants have been a bonus. If I had to retire again, this is what I would do.

SALLEYLAND FIELD NOTES, MAY 15, 2018

CAROLYN AND I PURCHASED THE INITIAL THIRTY-FIVE ACRES FOR Salleyland in 2008. We built the cabin in 2012 and bought an adjoining thirty-five acres in 2013. Susan Lane and Keith bought the adjacent thirty-five acres. Salleyland, named for the nearby town of Salley, quickly became our own Hundred Acre Wood, populated by a parade of Christopher Robins and friends.

Most, though not all, projects are more easily completed if you start with a plan. For our newly acquired land, I had an amorphous one that evolved into three general goals: enjoy all wildlife; inventory the herpetofauna; keep a record of wildlife experiences. Each had open-ended, shifting objectives, and all revolved around natural habitats and their inhabitants, not only the obvious plants and animals but also the hidden biodiversity that can easily go unseen. Examining nature by adjusting the lens I had used during my career as a research ecologist and data-collecting scientist revealed a new frontier, formerly unappreciated: a plot of land with its paradoxical mix of environmental simplicity and complexity. Any homeowner with a yard can experience the same emotions on a smaller scale. Any visitor to a municipal, state, or national park can as well.

Goal 1: Enjoy All Wildlife

Wildlife can be defined as any living things not managed by humans. As a herpetologist, I had a special interest in targeting reptiles and amphibians, but I knew untold treasures awaited across the wildlife spectrum at Salleyland. I was ready to see what I shared the land with and learn what I could about each inhabitant. That endeavor forms the basis for this book.

For the first two or three years, my grandchildren and I, along with anyone else we could recruit for a field trip, walked and boated, turned over rocks and logs, observed and recorded. We recorded whatever we found of interest. We set a few minnow traps in swamp pools and in the water along the edge of the creek, but hard-core collecting techniques used by professional ecologists were not part of our initial effort. Instead, we used materials that did not need a research grant to purchase. We also used only techniques that would not require constant checking, to make sure no animal died in a trap.

As a professional albeit retired herpetologist, I was particularly interested in compiling a list of reptiles and amphibians documented from the site (see appendix 1). A second goal was to augment the herpetofaunal list with inventories of the other vertebrate groups (mammals, birds, and fishes), as well as vascular plants and mushrooms. Aquatic, terrestrial, and aerial invertebrates such as clams, millipedes, spiders, dragonflies, and butterflies were included in the mix (see appendix 2). I also wanted to provide an overview of the geology and archaeological history of the site. So far, the plan has been successful and one shifting goal after another has been reached.

Philatelists collect stamps, numismatists collect coins, and some ecologists collect lists of species. Bird-watchers live for their next lifer, and the same has become true for some herpetologists. J. D. Willson, one of my former graduate students and an outstanding naturalist, once drove from Aiken, South Carolina, to Orlando, Florida, to see his first masked duck, a Mexican species that had been reported by bird-watchers to have landed on a lake in Florida. In later years, as a young professor at the University of Arkansas, J. D. took several of his students, my academic grandchildren, to southern Texas to see a tropical wading bird known as a jacana and a Texas indigo snake in the wild. Finding both on the first day, they turned around and drove to northern Minnesota to see an ivory gull, great gray owl, and gyrfalcon. I can't compete with such a record. I took one of my longest trips in search of reptiles when Mike turned sixteen. We flew from South Carolina to visit Randy Babb in Arizona. Our goal was to see how many different species of rattlesnakes we could find. Of the eleven Arizona rattlesnake species accepted by herpetologists to be valid at the time, we found nine. Successful trip! I repeated that trip when Parker was the same age Mike had been. We didn't catch as many kinds of rattlesnakes but we did find a Gila monster in the wild, an awesome lizard that had eluded us years before. Another successful trip.

The urge to make lists, from to-do lists to grocery lists to *The Book of Lists* is arguably an innate, ingrained human trait. Nonetheless, taxonomic list makers are viewed with disdain by many scientists who consider such activities a waste of time, contributing nothing to the advancement of science. I categorically disagree. To seek and find simply for the sake of saying you've seen what you seek is natural and normal human behavior. The evolutionary bedrock for such behavior is obvious. The more we know about wildlife and our natural surroundings, the greater opportunity we have of discovering something of value or avoiding a threat. Learning what plants and animals are around us indisputably falls within the realm of science. I set out to document the biodiversity within a prescribed area, and along the way I got others involved in exploring nature's secrets and discovering the mundane and the extraordinary.

Goal 2: Inventory the Herpetofauna

As a retired herpetologist, I particularly wanted to see how many different kinds of reptiles and amphibians I could find on the property, without the weightiness of having to take measurements, analyze the data, and eventually publish the findings in a scientific journal. I had published literally hundreds of scientific articles, figuratively enough to last a lifetime. Retirement was recess. I could find a snake, turtle, or salamander and simply enjoy having done so without further ado beyond, perhaps, a photograph and a field note. The experience was enhanced for me if someone else got to see my discovery too.

Once I realized I had a wide variety of native reptile and amphibian neighbors at Salleyland, a tangible objective became to keep a list of as many species of herpetofauna (reptiles and amphibians) as we could find. Documenting the distribution and abundance of reptiles and amphibians on a parcel of land seems to me like normal behavior. Having spent a good part of my fifty-year career conducting herpetofaunal surveys to develop species inventories for national parks, federal wildlife reserves, and US defense facilities, land areas totaling hundreds of square miles, I was confident I could compile a basic list of species on only a few acres.

I set up weekly, monthly, and yearly objectives. The need to document species found on the land bordered on an obsession for me and a few other participants. With each batch of new discoveries, we changed the goal. Find twenty species. Then thirty. Then forty. When the total reached fifty, I knew developing herpetofaunal inventories at Salleyland could last me a lifetime. I decided to implement search efforts to discover as many different reptiles and amphibians as possible while pursuing the plan of finding other wildlife on the land and learning about them as well.

Our small tract of land had many more reptiles and amphibians than I expected. At another site three decades earlier, with the help of dozens of students and other colleagues, I had conducted a survey documenting one hundred reptile and amphibian species, about two-thirds of the total in the state. The area surveyed was a protected defense facility (the Department of Energy's Savannah River Site) of a quarter million acres—more than twenty-five hundred times as large as my tract only thirty miles away. Having only those facts, an absurd mathematical calculation might be that my land should have no more than a single species. Anyone who has seen turtles basking on a log in a five-acre pond alongside a tree with a lizard on it while a bullfrog is booming alongshore would know the relationship between land area and species numbers is not linear. You must incorporate ecology, and hence biology, into the equation.

Ecology is more complex than math, chemistry, or physics because the variables are virtually unending. People should say "it's not ecology" instead of "it's not rocket science." Ecology, a subset of biology, has way more variables than any rocket launch. My questions at Salleyland became, how many of the hundred species found on a much larger land area only a few miles away would I find on my land, and what were they doing there?

Goal 3: Keep a Record

Shortly after we had built the cabin with a porch overlooking our blackwater stream, writing the story of Salleyland became tractable and enjoyable. No internet. Limited cell service. No interruptions by visitors, other than wildlife. The story was all around me and could be written without distraction.

I based much of this book on dated field notes recounting observations

The discovery of the first red salamander at Salleyland prompted us to start an inventory of reptiles and amphibians. Photo by Stephen Bennett.

or happenings when each new species or previously unreported natural phenomenon was discovered. The notes give in-depth information based on the scientific literature, discussions with experts (professional and amateur), and personal observation of the ecology of selected species or groups of organisms. I encouraged visitors to record their experiences at Salleyland in a guest log. These accounts reveal how they felt upon encountering the array of inhabitants on the land. Some encounters were expected, most came as a surprise. These visitors, like most people who experience nature's marvels firsthand, were captivated.

I set out to complete an inventory of the reptiles, amphibians, and other wildlife—which includes all animals, plants, and fungi—on the land. An equally important objective was to teach anyone interested in accompanying me in the woods, stream, swamp, and fields of Salleyland. As it turns out, I have learned far more about wildlife and ecology from our four hundred–plus visitors than I have taught them. In *Salleyland* I offer myriad ways in which anyone who enjoys nature can approach a tract of land, no matter how big or how small. Whether we are hosts or invitees, the living world is around us wherever we go and is waiting to reveal its secrets.

Meet Your Neighbors

We met some of our neighbors today—four new species of herps—one amphibian and three reptiles! Mike found a musk turtle shell and our first little brown skink rustling through the grass. Parker, Nick, and Allison boated upstream from the cabin and saw a red-bellied watersnake basking in smilax vines over the stream. We added a narrow-mouthed toad at the edge of the field under a rotten log.

SALLEYLAND FIELD NOTES, APRIL 13, 2013

WHEN MOVING INTO A NEW NEIGHBORHOOD YOU WANT TO MEET YOUR neighbors. Prior to the summer of 2012 my trips to the land were infrequent, averaging fewer than once a month and usually by myself. My journal entry from Salleyland on February 23, 2012, noted that one of the neighbors who lived across the dirt road from our property stopped by in his little white pickup truck. He was quite chatty and offered a great deal of information, mostly about my own activities.

He mentioned our putting up wood duck boxes the month before and asked if any ducks had nested yet. He wanted to know if we had caught any fish since we had put a boat in the stream last week. I nodded when he noted that the deer stand on the northeast side of the property was in disrepair and that our land was thirty-five acres. I continued to nod when he said a lady who co-owned the triangle of land east of us lived up the road. He also mentioned that he had lost a beagle. He allowed that he thought the man with property adjoining ours to the west shot dogs that ventured onto his land. He referred to him as a "mean man." The barrage of non sequiturs eventually ended with his asking if I would be interested in renting land for hunting rights, which I took to be his real objective for the visit. I said I would talk with him when deer season approached.

The exchange was instructive for me and, as it turned out, for him. I realized that the neighborhood watch program was in full operation as he had pin-pointed specific activities and had checked the county property records to see what we had bought. He was also intimating that he knew our land well and had probably hunted on it when it was no-man's-land and had who knows how many deer stands scattered about. This discussion also gave me the opportunity to mention that a wildlife camera (which he did not know about, in contrast to the duck box he had seen us put out and the boat he had watched us launch) had photographed his beagle. I noticed a flash of mindfulness when he realized cameras might be anywhere on our property and would pick up anything or anyone that triggered them. I told him the general area where the beagle was photographed, as well as the date and time. I didn't mention that the next animal seen on that very camera a few minutes later was a full-grown bobcat, our first record of one, following the same path as the beagle. Maybe the mean man had not shot his puppy dog after all.

Our pickup-driving neighbors are scarce compared to those that do not drive—and they have fascinating stories to tell.

Meeting the First Reptile

The first reptile species I saw on our newly acquired land, before I had decided to keep records, was a yellow-bellied slider turtle also known as a pond slider. I had studied the ecology of the species for decades and even written a book about them. As I watched from the bridge, two sliders slid off a log into the creek that bisected our initial thirty-five acres. I was glad to see them but not particularly impressed. Southern streams and wetlands are supposed to have slider turtles in them.

The first notable animal I saw was neither reptile nor amphibian. It was a large, distinctive bird. Even with my nascent ornithological skills I could identify it by both its call and its appearance. I had parked my little gray Ford Ranger on the road shoulder and was looking upstream. I heard it first and then saw the distinctive red, black, and white—a pileated woodpecker, the prototype of Woody Woodpecker.

Pileated woodpeckers belong to a taxonomic family of birds comprising more than two hundred species. With its dazzling red crest; loud, laughing call; and a body almost as big as a crow, the pileated is a magnificent fowl. It was often called a redheaded hen in the parts of Alabama where I grew up. Descriptive regional monikers are discouraged by the National Audubon Society and bird people who want set-in-stone names for each bird species. Ironically, these are the same people who change a few of the names every year, which keeps people like me from looking like they know bird names. The pileated is the bird that keeps alive unsubstantiated rumors that ivory-billed woodpeckers are not extinct. Supposed sightings of ivory bills are assumed by most ornithologists to have been pileated woodpeckers.

Representatives of woodpeckers occur on most major land masses of the world except for Australia and Madagascar. Characteristically, woodpeckers

Sam admires an adult ringneck snake, the most commonly found species of snake at Salleyland. Photo by Jennifer G. High.

have strong beaks for chiseling into trees and extremely long tongues for reaching into crevices for insects. Most have four toes on each foot, a pair pointing forward and another pair pointing backward, serving to brace the bird on vertical tree trunks. After hearing and seeing the pileated, I felt a thrill as I watched its flight from a dead loblolly pine to a sweetgum on the opposite side of the creek. It apparently was as happy as I was, for it was laughing all the way. Pileateds are one of my favorite birds, and with the putative extinction of the ivory-bill are now the largest North American woodpecker. Their large nest holes in dead pines as well as hardwoods and the chunks of wood they knock from trees when searching for food are impressive by-products of their presence. I noticed a few chiseled-out squares high in the dead pine where I assumed a pileated had been flushing out a prevalent item in its diet—carpenter ants. Perhaps an even more remarkable aspect of the natural history of this enormous bird is a report more than a half century ago by an observant naturalist (F. K. Truslow). As he watched from a blind, he saw and photographed a female pileated woodpecker pick up her eggs one at a time in her mouth and transport them away from a tree hole after the tree broke and exposed the nest.

Just as this feathered marvel landed in the sweetgum, another bird caught my eye, an even larger one, circling high above. I knew it was a raptor of some sort, and its high-pitched call similar to a blue jay identified it as a red-shouldered hawk. It continued its lazy drifting, ultimately disappearing upstream beyond the swamp forest of red maple and tupelo gum trees in the floodplain of the creek. I knew I would soon discover other birds, smaller and less impressive. These two seemed like heralds proclaiming the promise of ecological adventures to come. Clearly, exploration was on the agenda. I left the road and headed into the woods.

Meeting the First Mammal

I experienced two other memorable wildlife events on my first day: a third bird and a mammal. With a machete I had brought from the truck, I cut and pushed my way through roadside brush of Carolina cherry laurel, honeysuckle, and greenbrier vines to reach the edge of the mixed oak-hickory hardwood forest with occasional tall pine trees. A sparse understory of small oaks, hollies, sparkleberry, and flowering dogwoods was ever present. With the tangled barrier of shrubs and vines gone, left by the roadside, I now walked through an open and inviting forest. Cutting a trail was no longer necessary. A mild euphoria came over me. I owned a small woodland that I could access at any time. I became aware of a creeping sense of that primordial behavior I had not experienced since we had bought our house with its big back yard many years ago—territoriality. I wandered around the land for an hour, seeing plenty of small birds as well as trees and mushrooms I could only identify in the most generic terms—a warbler, an oak, or, in the case of mushrooms, pink, yellow, or white. I resolved to bring out former colleagues who were ecologists and trained specialists in various taxonomic fields. They could identify the birds, plants, and mushrooms for me.

The woods were on a slope I later determined went from the creek at an elevation of about two hundred feet above sea level to a plateau at the top at over three hundred feet. I continued the journey to the top, eventually deciding I had reached the boundary of the adjoining property. Assuming the owners might have a hint of territoriality of their own and not knowing exactly where the property line was, I turned to go down. As I descended toward the creek, the woods were still open and easily navigable until I encountered a green barrier with yellow trimming. I recognized a canebrake, a microhabitat composed of a single species of plant in the genus of North America's only native bamboo. I called it switch cane growing up in Alabama, but some authorities consider more acceptable terminology to be river cane or just plain cane, depending on which botanist you talk to. According to Steven Platt, an authority on the genus *Arundinaria*, large stands were once common. Now they are another disappearing ecosystem of the Southeast.

Each plant stood erect, the tallest stalk not much over six feet. Thin branches pointed upward, ending in a cluster of elongate green leaves. Some of the leaves were tan, leftovers from what I assumed was a natural death during fall and winter. In our area new leaf growth appears in the spring. The canebrake extended up- and downstream in the floodplain of the creek as far as I could see in either direction. I was pleased to see we had our own little monoculture along the creek at Salleyland.

As I emerged from the canebrake with the creek in front of me, I heard the sound of another of the few birds I, or anyone, would recognize—wood ducks. The whistles and squeaks of departing wood ducks are unlikely to be confused with any other in the Southeast. This pair created splashes as they left the creek and flew away downstream. A male wood duck in breeding plumage may be the most beautiful bird in North America. It is surely one of the finest examples of natural art in the animal kingdom with its Mondrian-like plumage of red, green, brown, tan, black, white, and blue. The species was the tenth to be featured on the Federal Duck Stamp (1943–44). Wood ducks appeared again on these iconic stamps in 1974–75, 2012–13, and again in 2019–20. I stood transfixed as the pair rocketed away above the water along the tree-lined far side of the creek. I could still hear them in the distance when I heard another sound, one less familiar to me in a bottom-land swamp forest—tinkling water. I did not need the expertise of any of my mammalogist colleagues to tell me I had stumbled onto a beaver dam, one of the few origins of a waterfall once a stream leaves the Piedmont and flows onto the Coastal Plain.

Parker (*left*) examines a chubsucker while Nick marvels at a
slider turtle caught in the creek. Photo by author.

I did not see a beaver that day, but I knew without doubt that I had beavers as neighbors in my creek, yet another wildlife treasure to be appreciated. I headed back to my truck walking parallel to the creek outside the ribbon of switch cane, inspired by the notion of owning the land where they all lived and being able to have friends and family enjoy it with me.

Meeting the First Amphibian

Parker found the first amphibian. Both Parker and the baby slimy salamander were little tykes at the time. I wanted to show Mike and Parker the new property and had hopes we would find something of interest in the way of a reptile or amphibian. The salamander was under a log Parker turned over on the wooded hillside. A green tiger beetle caught my eye as it scurried into the leaves next to the log, which I used as my excuse for not seeing the black salamander with white spots that Parker pointed at. He had seen salamanders before during educational outreach talks I had given at his school, but this was his first experience seeing one in the wild.

Slimy salamanders are a hallmark of healthy woodlands throughout much of the eastern United States. In contrast to salamanders in other families, they are fully terrestrial, laying eggs on land instead of in aquatic habitats. The family they belong to, Plethodontidae, are the lungless salamanders, which breathe through their skin. A slimy salamander is aptly named because of a viscous gluelike material covering the skin. Even the original scientific name, *Plethodon glutinosus*, is true to the trait, as glutinous means gluelike. When Mike and I encouraged Parker to pick up his first slimy salamander, he quickly learned that the slime sticks to your hand like an epoxy resin but causes no irritation. Before the salamander could dry out from being handled, we returned it to its damp home beneath the log and carefully covered it with its roof, the log itself.

Following the slimy salamander as the first amphibian came the second amphibian and first frog. The bronze frog turned out to be the most common frog at Salleyland, being the most seen and most heard every year. Closely related to and similar in appearance to the bullfrog, bronze frogs are readily distinguishable from bullfrogs as soon as they metamorphose because of a single characteristic: a visible ridge running down each side of the back from behind the eye almost to the groin area. A bullfrog has a completely smooth back and sides. In addition a bullfrog has a booming bellow of a mating call that can be heard a quarter-mile away. A male bronze frog makes a short "bonk" sound, like one pluck of a banjo. We have found bronze frogs at Salleyland in every month, usually under logs or coverboards in the swamp, and heard them from March to September, usually at night but sometimes during the day. We do not hear them call in large choruses like southern leopard frogs, green treefrogs, spring peepers, or southern toads on the property. Seldom are more than half a dozen bronze frogs heard at the same time, and these are usually spaced apart a hundred feet or more along the creek or in the swamp. But they are always around.

For Salleyland's visiting herpetologists, the most intriguing salamander to find is one of the smallest salamanders on the continent, Chamberlain's dwarf salamander. Few people, including herpetologists, have ever seen one in the wild because of their localized distribution, small size, and clandestine behavior. They hide beneath leaves, logs, and other natural cover most of their lives. I think my first sight of one at Salleyland was in May 2014 during a visit from Will Dillman, at the time the state herpetologist with South Carolina's Department of Natural Resources. The day was warm and pleasant, nowhere near the insufferable heat and humidity of a typical day in August.

As we walked from the cabin into the swamp, we moved through lush vegetation of almost chest-high cinnamon ferns and royal ferns reminiscent of a primordial wetland. Will caught a young rat snake crawling over the ground, and as he released it, he stirred some leaves at the base of a tree with his snake stick. Reaching down, he picked up a tiny yellowish salamander less than two inches long, yet an adult. We felt certain it was one of the dwarf salamanders, but when he handed it to me, it jumped out of my hand, disappearing in the wet, heavily vegetated floor of the swamp. A brief search was futile. We had missed our opportunity to confirm our observation by counting the toes on its back feet. Dwarf salamanders have only four on each hind foot whereas most similar-looking species have five.

Fortunately, Steve Bennett, the former state herpetologist of South Carolina, whose position Will had taken when Steve retired, confirmed the presence of Chamberlain's dwarf salamander in the Salleyland sphagnum swamp by catching one the following month. We brought it safely to the cabin and examined it with a hand lens. Four toes on each back foot! Steve and Will still argue about who caught the first one at Salleyland because we don't know for sure that what Will found was a Chamberlain's dwarf salamander. I remain ambivalent about who caught the first one, which is why I say, "I *think* my first sight of one. . . ." I can state unequivocally that I can take no credit for either.

Always Good to Find a Cottonmouth

I added the second reptile to my list as I stood on the highway bridge in early May 2010 waiting for Steve Bennett to arrive from Columbia. I looked upstream and saw a female slider turtle's head motionless in the water alongside the fallen tree it had slid off when I arrived. I knew it was a female because of its large size and the bright yellow wash on its head. Male sliders do not get as large, and older males lose the yellow color characteristic of juveniles and females. I peered down into the black water, which would look like clear spring water if poured into a glass. Blackwater streams in the region appear dark because of organic sediments. But I didn't need to see below the surface to register the newcomer. I saw the thick, spear-shaped head as it emerged from beneath the leaves of a green arrow arum plant growing along the shore. As the rest of the snake's thick body glided into view, identification became indisputable. It was a large cottonmouth. Its apparent goal was to cross the creek, and being unaware of my presence several feet above on the bridge, it languidly undulated toward the border of pondweed on the other side. It moved gracefully, head held imperiously above the water's surface.

Cottonmouths swim with their upper surface above the water, so I could see the olive-brown body with darker crossbands at intervals of a few inches. I glanced up the road in hopes of seeing Steve so we could both enjoy watching one of the Southeast's iconic snakes. Unnecessarily feared by many residents of the region, its greatest fault is to have made a liar out of many of them. Based on a scientific study conducted on cottonmouths in the wild, the fact is that these large venomous serpents do not chase people. Normally they do not even bite unless picked up or aggravated beyond their tolerance. Yet an amazing number of southerners will tell you a different tale, swearing they are aggressive. When threatened, a cottonmouth will sit with open mouth (which is as white as Alabama cotton) as a don't-tread-on-me warning. I have encountered hundreds of cottonmouths and I have never been chased. I haven't even been struck at when standing only inches away.

The snake was halfway across the creek, leaving a sinuous ripple in its wake, when I saw Steve's pickup truck coming down the road. I gave a hurry-up wave so he drove to the edge of the bridge and jumped out. I pointed to the last waves as the snake entered the vegetation. I started to explain what Steve had missed when I was spared the need. The vegetation parted inches away from where the big cottonmouth had entered and out came a slightly

smaller one, moving fast toward the opposite bank. Cottonmouths are no-
torious predators of smaller snakes of any kind and are confirmed cannibals
on their own species. Cottonmouths may not go after people, but the smaller
snake, swimming as fast as it could, knew that the new arrival would go after
it if given the opportunity. I added the new species to our wildlife list.

Amphibians Keep on Coming

Steve and I recorded three more species that day, two salamanders, one frog.
Salleyland would prove to be home to at least ten different kinds of salamanders, some of which most herpetologists have never seen in the wild. The
first was an inappropriately named animal, the mud salamander. Naming
an animal after dark, wet, yucky sediment is fitting for the brown-colored
eastern mud minnow we caught in a dip net, but not for the marvelous little red-bodied salamander that peered at us questioningly with coal-black
eyes. Some mud salamanders have the red-leopard appearance of a related
species aptly called a red salamander, but the latter has yellow irises. Staring
down a salamander is not that hard to do, so Steve and I knew which one
we had caught.

We continued to poke around in the swamp mud and vegetation and
out scurried a long-tailed yellow salamander with distinct black stripes running the length of its slender body—a three-lined salamander. Over the
years, three-lined salamanders would become the most frequently encountered amphibians in the swamp and along the stream margins. Larvae of
mud salamanders and three-lined salamanders have gills and are aquatic.
The adults lose their gills, but both stay in wet areas, acquiring oxygen
through their skin like the more terrestrial slimy salamander, which is in
the same family. Anyone with an appreciation of natural beauty marvels at
the vibrant yellow of a three-lined salamander against a backdrop of swamp
mud. The bright yellow topside contrasts sharply with the salamander's underside: a black-and-white reticulated network that generally evokes an ex-
clamation from someone observing it for the first time. Turning small creatures upside down can reveal colors and patterns completely different from
their topsides.

As we were leaving, Steve stopped and held a hand up for me to listen. From the wooded area across the stream I heard it too. The melodious
trill of a Cope's gray treefrog. These robust little treefrogs call from trees
during the warmer months, both day and night. Most are dark or pale gray

with a pattern that looks like lichens on an oak tree. The species is a text-book example of the use of flash colors, a special defense for some animals. The gray treefrog is a perfectly camouflaged creature when sitting on an oak tree or other drab background, especially a tree trunk with patches of lichens. When a gray treefrog is pursued by a bird intent on making a meal of it, however, the frog jumps, displaying a wash of bright yellow underparts. When it lands on a tree and tucks in its legs, the frog again blends into the background. The bird, meanwhile, searches for something yellow that it can no longer see.

The skin secretions of a gray treefrog can irritate eyes, nasal membranes, and open cuts. Washing with soap and water readily removes the irritant. Many years ago in a swamp at night, I did not wash my hands after catch-ing a gray treefrog. Then I rubbed my eyes. The burning sensation was so intense that I asked the people with me to stop the van alongside a stream so I could rinse my eyes out—not the most sanitary solution but better than doing nothing.

My mantra regarding animals is that you want to experience them. You need not catch them or even see them. Smelling the unmistakable odor of a skunk counts as experiencing a skunk. Hearing an animal you can positively identify also counts. Therefore, the gray treefrog Steve and I heard qualified as our fifth herp species. We added it to the inventory list. After that first ID by sound in 2010, we have heard them more than fifty times—phantom music in the tall trees. They are all around us, but no one has yet held one in hand at Salleyland, which for me may be a good thing.

A Notable Find

Finding an adult red salamander, the closest relative to the mud salamander, which can also be red, is a bonus on any field trip. The home site for both species as larvae is the wet and muddy swamp. After losing their gills and metamorphosing, mud salamanders remain in wet habitats and mud. The more adventurous red salamanders head for higher ground.

I had no expectation of seeing a red salamander at Salleyland, but for-tunately Steve had driven his South Carolina Department of Natural Re-sources pickup truck with its SCDNR name and logo on the door. When he left that day he felt comfortable taking ungated dirt roads across other people's property and following the powerline right-of-way till he got to the north end of Salleyland. I had only been there once.

I might have questioned the validity of a red salamander sighting without some kind of backup verification. But Steve knows his salamanders. Plus, he sent an exquisite photo of the red salamander he had found. Its yellow eyes distinguished it from the brown-eyed mud salamander The day was a notable one for me because following such an exciting find was when I decided to keep a record of herpetofauna on Salleyland. Maybe we had more different kinds than I had first thought. Making a list of them would be a gratifying exercise.

Write It Down

There's nothing in this world quite like drinkin' a cup of coffee while pulling traps in the morning, watching fireflies blinking over a dark, midnight creek as whip-poor-wills call and lightning flashes and friends ooh and aah. These wonderland memories are lifelong.

JULIANA SMITH, SALLEYLAND GUEST LOG, SC
HERP SOCIETY BIOBLITZ, MAY 5, 2019

Salleyland is a wonderful, magical place! We had an incredible time and created stories I will remember for the rest of my life. Thanks to Parker for showing me my first mud snake!!

JAKE ZADIK, SALLEYLAND GUEST LOG, SC
HERP SOCIETY BIOBLITZ, MAY 5, 2019

ON MONDAY MAY 3, 2010, I BEGAN WRITING DAILY FIELD NOTES OF every trip to Salleyland. Although I had kept sporadic field notes and recorded each new reptile or amphibian species when we found it, most were of random encounters as we wandered aimlessly around the property during occasional trips to the land. Few visits were made before 2012 when we decided to build a cabin, which led to more frequent trips to the land.

Regardless of how significant an adventure or discovery seems at the time, time itself will blur the memory, intertwine it with others, sometimes erase it entirely. Documenting the experience—with written notes on paper or computer; with an audio or video recording—will keep the record permanent and accurate. The following suggestions are meant for anyone who enjoys spending time outdoors in natural settings, no matter where that setting might be.

Take Field Notes

One need not be retired to discover the pleasure of taking field notes. I have long recommended that teachers and parents encourage children to keep records of their outdoor nature experiences. I found a spiral-bound notebook in an old box in my office and was reminded that I took my first field notes in 1954, when I was fifteen. Reading that notebook was like opening a time capsule. "Most of the time it was raining heavily and later hailed. . . . Bob Helms and I collected at Lake Wildwood near Tuscaloosa, Alabama." That entry was dated April 15, 1956. A few pages earlier the entry noted that I "collected at Payne's Prairie south of Gainesville, Florida." The date for the Florida trip was October 18, 1955.

I had rediscovered my notes taken on nature field trips from when I was in high school. Both of those entries listed who was with me and what we caught, which included twelve lizards and seven snakes for the rainy day in Alabama. The Florida trip yielded the first eastern kingsnake I had ever caught, or even seen. The notes were handwritten in India ink, the indelible ink used by scientists and young wannabe scientists of the time to take permanent notes that were to last forever. For me, that system has worked just fine for well over a half century. Children interested in developing ideas for stories or just remembering what they said to whom and when they said it may want to keep a diary. But for boys and girls who love nature and the outdoors, a field notebook is the way to go.

Adults who enjoy outdoor excursions, whether near home or far away, can benefit from taking field notes. When I taught college classes, I required my students to take copious notes on field trips. Our powers of misremembering events is much greater than we like to admit. Writing down details when they are fresh is the only sure way to know your recollections are accurate. Teach a child how to take nature field notes. Fifty years from now they will be glad you did.

One simple technique for taking nature notes is to ask six questions that journalists ask: who, what, why, where, when, and how. Start the entry by noting where you were as precisely as possible and when you were there (date and time). Who you were with will be important if you later need to check a fact or confirm a memory. As you get older, remembering friends and colleagues with whom you had a particular adventure becomes more meaningful—and more difficult. A written record will help you recall people and events.

If you are on a quest for wild plants or animals, what you saw, heard, and smelled are critical bits of information. Touch might be part of the experience. Taste also, but only if you know exactly what you are tasting. If you caught or observed something, record what and where it was and how you found it. Hiding under a log? Basking on a rock? Crawling across the path? A description of the weather is always important ecologically. The why question may get a bit iffier. Although some excursions are undertaken for a specific reason, it's always acceptable to walk around in the woods just because you can.

Start an Environmental Journal

Field notes are what I call the daily record describing what you did and saw on any given day. John Byrd, an outstanding educator in Tennessee who has visited Salleyland many times, has his students keep an environmental journal. This exercise addresses several educational goals—to hone writing skills, communicate observations and ideas, and learn to think environmentally. His suggestions for journal entries include recording what you've observed, asking questions, writing poetry or stories, and summarizing information gained from books and other sources. An environmental journal would also be a suitable assignment for some language arts classes.

The most straightforward way to make an environmental journal is to record your observations, including animal behavior and patterns of flowering among plants. You might note how many different kinds of pollinators (bees, flies, beetles, etc.) are attracted to fall-blooming plants. A bewildering array of wasps, some strikingly colored, buzz around composites (such as goldenrods, dog fennel, and ironweed) that flower in late summer and early autumn. Watching wasps from a safe distance is an entertaining exercise and could be worth recording in one's field notes and expanding upon in a journal. Small groups of students might work together to record observations in the schoolyard. Having various students read aloud from their field notes or environmental journals about the same trip demonstrates how different eyes and ears interpret the same outing.

Asking questions is always worthwhile. Why do some birds, like Carolina wrens, stay around all year and sing in every month? Whereas others, like most warblers, migrate, going south in the fall and north in the spring. And some resident birds sing seasonally. Why are moths and scarab beetles attracted to lights at night? Why do most oak trees, hickories, and sweetgums lose all their leaves in the fall, but live oaks, hollies, and pine trees stay green year-round? These and countless other ecological questions may not have simple answers. Exceptions to the rule, whatever it is, will be rampant and bring universally accepted scientific explanations into question. And some questions remain unanswered. Nonetheless, look for answers from a reliable source, preferably a scientific paper, biology textbook, or trusted academic website. Make it a goal to consider a question that scientists have not yet answered satisfactorily. For example, why are female hawks and owls usually larger than males? Many scientific answers and explanations have been offered for this question, but no single one is agreed upon by ornithologists.

Another suggestion is to write an environmental poem or even a short story (with emphasis on "short" if a teacher has to read it or a class has to listen to it). Do these activities on days you can't get out to observe and can't come up with a biological question that intrigues you.

> In woods and fields of summer's green
> Bugs abound as I have seen.
> When winter's brown is near and far,
> I can but wonder where they are.

Not sure what kind of grade I might get for that verse, but it would provide a jumping-off point for a discussion of the life cycle of insects. Or how about a short story told by a rabbit that has just left its hiding place under a bush and encountered a bobcat?

Making lists of what plants and animals you see during a walk around your own neighborhood can reveal how diverse the local environment is. You might categorize the flora and fauna you've observed into taxonomic categories and then gather natural history information about them from reliable sources. This provides an open-ended opportunity for anyone to learn about their natural surroundings. Elementary, middle, and high school teachers should consider incorporating ecology into lesson plans to cultivate students' appreciation for nature. Going outside to observe plants, animals, and the habitats they live in is a suitable exercise for science classes from grammar school through college. Teachers invariably find that students take great interest in observing the living world. Having them write down their observations makes an excellent follow-up exercise.

You need not be in school to keep an environmental journal. Anyone exploring a natural habitat can write down their observations then turn those journal entries into short essays or poems. Nature is all around us and the more we know about our environment the better. Imagine finding some natural phenomenon that has hitherto gone unnoticed. That would be exciting. But you can enjoy being outdoors, observing and wondering, without making such discoveries. Reading your entries a year or more afterward can be enlightening. Keeping an environmental journal can help you develop or enhance your appreciation of nature. You might encourage others to do so as well. Without question a journal will provide enjoyable reading opportunities that will last a lifetime.

Have a Guest Log

One's memory and reality do not always agree, often following different paths. Taking field notes each day keeps events in order. Sometimes embellished memories make for better stories. But when you need the facts—such as when did we start building the cabin? who was with me when we caught the first kingsnake (John Byrd; Herp species #46) at Salleyland? who caught the first queen snake (Parker; Herp species #55)—notes are invaluable. I also keep a record of dates various people have visited. To have visitors record their own thoughts gives an additional perspective. To this end, we set up a notebook at the cabin for people to say something about their experience at Salleyland.

The number of people who have visited Salleyland is much greater than the number of entries in the guest book. In a visiting college class, many students simply do not get around to it without some urging by the instructor or me. In addition, I do not want someone's comments when they arrive. What are they supposed to say? "Hey, nice cabin" or "pretty view of the stream from the porch." More meaningful comments can be made after they have seen, heard, smelled, tasted, or touched something noteworthy to them, especially if it was their first such experience. However, when someone is getting ready to leave they are often making sure they haven't forgotten anything or saying goodbye or taking one last photo. I now ask visitors to put their car keys between the pages of the guest notebook so they will remember to write something before leaving. Sometimes this means a trip back to the cabin from their vehicle to get the keys—and to write in the book. As long as the stimulus for leaving was not an imminent thunderstorm, the system works fine.

Once visitors are shown how to hold crawdads, most of them can
be persuaded to pick one up. Photo by Jermaine Frazier.

Record Spoor

The email message was short, "You may add *Lontra canadensis* to your mammal list!" I was delighted. *Lontra canadensis* is the scientific name of the river otter, and the message meant we had successfully used spoor to identify the seventeenth terrestrial mammal on our land. Learning to read spoor can make an ordinary trip through the woods, along a road, or beside a wetland more interesting year-round.

Many people like making lists of one sort or another. As an ecologist, I particularly enjoy knowing what plants and animals are around me outdoors. In the woods and wetlands of Salleyland, I compile biological inventories for my own edification, not as part of a scientific study. Keeping a list of wildlife species is a gratifying exercise. At one milestone in 2015 we had recorded eighteen species of amphibians, twenty-eight types of reptiles, and thirty-eight kinds of trees. Adding each newly discovered species to the master list gives me a feeling of accomplishment and makes me eager to find the next one in each category. I appreciated adding a cool creature like a river otter to our mammal list.

I relied on spoor to document the presence of river otters at the land. "Spoor" is a quirky word that in the broadest sense means an environmental clue to the past that has been left by an animal. For example, although snow is a rare commodity at Salleyland, once when we had a light dusting I found parallel, finger-length footprints on the hillside in the woods. Without question, a cottontail rabbit had been there. I did not have to be an experienced wildlife tracker to even be able to say how long ago—thirty minutes. Simple calculation—the thin layer of snow had only covered the ground for that long. You can also use olfactory spoor. An overpowering, pungent smell along a highway reveals that someone has crossed paths with a skunk, which probably met its demise as roadkill. Scat (animal fecal dropping) offers especially valuable environmental clues about unseen wildlife because each animal's scat is different from others. River otters use readily identifiable latrines.

A sure way to know that otters are around without actually seeing one is to find one of their latrines, which they return to on a regular basis. Otter latrines are neither yucky nor stinky. They consist mostly of a pile of crushed mollusk shells and fish scales, and maybe a few small bones. When Parker and I found such a pile on a ridge along our stream, he immediately said "otter." I concurred but wanted confirmation from an expert. I contacted Leslie Ruyle, who has conducted extensive otter ecology studies. She took one look at the photo, validated our ID, and sent me the email confirming the presence of river otters at Salleyland.

Sophisticated instrumentation of all sorts is now available for ecological studies. Radiotelemetry can tell us where animals go. Radiography and sonography may be used to determine how many eggs an animal is carrying. A college student studying reptiles in a lake recently showed me a video of swimming and basking turtles that had been taken from a drone he was operating. Such gadgetry can unquestionably be a valuable tool for studying nature. But learning to recognize basic environmental clues allows anyone to enjoy nature with no store-bought accoutrements. Gadgetry should not obviate observation.

Sometimes even the simplest environmental clues can tell us something about wildlife in the world around us. Finding the mud tower surrounding a crawfish hole, seeing a tree that has been girdled by a beaver, identifying the readily recognizable footprint of a raccoon on a muddy creek bank all offer wildlife experiences that let us know we have company. We do not need to see, hear, or smell the animal itself to confirm that we are not alone.

I will continue to enjoy nature in the old-school way by looking for spoor in the form of tracks and other signs. But I appreciate technology. We got further documentation of our river otters by using a more modern approach. Assuming the otters visited the latrine by our creek on a regular basis, we set up a wildlife camera along the ridge where Parker found the latrine. Sure enough, the next night we got a picture of a river otter coming out of the stream. Sometimes you need to combine the old and the new to get the full picture.

Document a Presence

What do a turtle shell on the shoreline, a shed snakeskin beneath ground litter, and a distant frog call deep in the swamp have in common? All qualify as evidence of the documented presence of a particular species—at Salleyland or elsewhere. A canon of environmental education on field trips is to have participants embrace the idea of "experiencing the species" in ways other than just seeing it or catching it. The song of a white-eyed vireo, which sounds like something from R2-D2's playbook, gives sufficient evidence of the presence of the species without your catching sight of the bird. We have heard the door-knocking call of the yellow-billed cuckoo many times at Salleyland, but I have only seen one up close. As all bird-watchers understand, when you hear the sound you have experienced the bird. You don't have to see it to know it's around; likewise, you don't have to hear it if you see it. You can also record the white-eyed vireo as present without ever seeing or hearing it if you find and identify its nest, framed and initially supported by collected spiderwebs and caterpillar silk. Finding a blue jay, barred owl, or wild turkey feather on the ground is acceptable evidence that the bird is around. Wild turkeys also make distinctive ground scrapings in search of under-the-leaves prey. You can experience animals in many ways.

In compiling our inventory of reptiles and amphibians, our first record of a common musk turtle, also aptly called a stinkpot, was an empty shell. We expected to find these little fist-size, bottom-feeding, gray-brown denizens in stream and swamp. Once Mike found the shell, we knew musk turtles were present, and we began dipnetting and setting turtle traps in that area. We verified not only their existence but also their abundance as part of the herpetofauna of Salleyland. Sam found the shed skin of what I thought was a scarlet snake under a tin coverboard. I showed the skin to three herpetologists who confirmed my identification of a scarlet snake, a small and beautiful red, black, and white southeastern species that is active only at night. Only a novice who had never looked in a reptile field guide would mistake this red-nosed little creature for the venomous coral snake with its black nose. But my guess is that more than a few scarlet snakes have been killed because of someone's ignorance. I placed the species on the snake list with an asterisk, awaiting verification with a live individual.

The asterisk remained for a year and a month, until SCAN (South Carolina Association of Naturalists) spent a weekend at Salleyland. One group found a scarlet snake under a coverboard in the woods but released it before I ever saw it. Fortunately, that night two of the naturalists set out to find one. Many snakes are nocturnal at times. Scarlet snakes are the only one in the Southeast that come out exclusively at night. A scarlet snake found in the daytime is virtually always under a log or rock. Greg Ross and Mike Martin found one that night actively crawling in the field near the same coverboard where Sam had found the shed skin. Spoor evidence verified; asterisk removed.

Some animals, particularly certain mammals and birds, leave plenty of clues to their presence. Scrapings on a sapling by budding autumn antlers or the emblematic hoof print in the dirt at any time provide evidence of white-tailed deer. A freshly cut and skinned sweetgum branch with clear toothmarks at either end floating in the creek is sure sign of beaver activity, as well as the unequivocal evidence of a beaver dam. An easily observed trail of disturbed, upturned dead leaves of oak and hickory, punctuated by hand-size holes from the diggings of a long snout, soon become recognizable to anyone as the handiwork of an armadillo. All these clues indicated the presence of each species at Salleyland; personal sightings soon followed.

Name Your Places

Ownership can mean you have legal possession of something. It can also indicate an emotional state based on familiarity and affection. Anyone who frequently visits the same place, whether public grounds or private property, will develop a sense of appreciation not evident on their first visit. A natural tendency soon reveals itself—to give names to identifiable features of the landscape like distinctive rock formations, frequently used trails, notable trees, or dilapidated remnants of old wooden structures. A practical aspect is to be able to tell others where the location of something is. "Go down the Lake Trail till you get to the Big Loblolly."

Naming places is a form of territoriality. Some place-names change with the government. Bombay has become Mumbai. Sri Lanka was once Ceylon. Thailand has replaced Siam. Some geographical designations remain as adjectives although the country names have disappeared, for example, Burmese pythons, Siamese cats, and Persian rugs. Changing a company's name is one of the first steps following a corporate takeover.

We quickly began naming areas of Salleyland. Carolyn dubbed the lane leading to the cabin SNAP Road, for Sam, Nick, Allison, and Parker. The Green Rug was a twenty-by-twenty-foot piece of AstroTurf from an abandoned campsite near the Big Sweetgum. The Rattlesnake Tree and Rattlesnake Stump, which are a half mile apart, remind us of experiences with large canebrake rattlesnakes. And at the Beehives, of course, you will find our bees.

Take Photographs

Cell phones with cameras have revolutionized social interactions. They have also become an excellent means of establishing regional patterns of abundance and diversity among plants and animals. *Amphibians and Reptiles of Georgia* is one the most comprehensive and reliable state field guides because senior editor John Jensen used citizen science records to establish where species occur in the state. Reports by laypeople of a reptile or amphibian where it has not been previously documented by a professional herpetologist are seldom held to be credible. However, when someone sent John a photograph to accompany the account, the record could be accepted as valid even if that snake, salamander, or toad had never before been reported from that county. Cell phone wildlife photography has revolutionized ecology and scientists' understanding of animal distribution patterns.

On a field trip always have a camera at the ready. Even people who have no interest in field trips per se can enjoy seeing a photo of beautiful Palamedes swallowtails swarming the pink blooms of wild piedmont azalea bushes. People's attitudes about natural habitats may be influenced by pictures and videos showcasing Mother Nature. The more people who champion environmental sanctity, the better for the environment. Wildlife photographs can make people want to be champions.

A new species for Salleyland, a striped mud turtle, requires careful inspection to confirm its identity. Photo by Mike Gibbons.

Having an ever-present camera at Salleyland has led to the identification of hundreds of plants, mushrooms, and insects. Having flower or lizard in hand is better than a photo when using a field guide. But if the plant, animal, or mushroom is not available later, having photos is far better than a verbal description. An essential first step in learning about an organism is identifying it. Having a thorough grasp of the basic biology of an organism leads to the satisfying mindset of ecological ownership.

Professional wildlife photographers are a boon for chronicling what you have. Having a gallery of wildlife pictures, even amateurish ones, from a particular site can alert visitors to what they might see. A photo collection of flowering plants, macroinvertebrates, and fishes can introduce guests to local or regional flora and fauna. At Salleyland we have a photo book for each of the major taxonomic groups of animals, plants, and mushrooms All photographs are taken on-site.

A camera also lets you keep a record of the people who accompany you on your adventures. Some of the most memorable photographs from field trips will be those taken of you and the people with you. Your photo of a beaver dam, coiled rattlesnake, or stand of flowering goldenrod might be useful in describing what you saw on the field trip. Photos of who was with you and what they looked like back then will become treasures as the decades pass. After a much shorter time, no one much will care about the dam, the snake, or the flower, as everyone can find photos of them.

Enjoy Every Season

Springtime rocks! Sam and I added a new species today—a beautiful coachwhip about 5 feet long under tin. I managed to let it escape into the blackberry bushes, but we got a good look. Sam did a great job learning the damselflies. We saw ebony jewelwings, variable dancers with their purple bodies, and one male duckweed firetail. By the time we left, Sam was able to identify them all.

Salleyland Field Notes, May 25, 2017

Plants and animals are all about time. Light, temperature, and moisture influence most of them. These physical aspects of natural environments are in most instances a function of time: day and night, lunar cycles, seasons of the year. Some animals and a few plants are active mostly at night, others only during daylight. Animal examples are easy to come by. Coachwhip snakes, as well as most birds and butterflies, are diurnal. Bats, moths, and scarlet snakes are primarily nocturnal. One noteworthy plant, the evening primrose, unfurls from bud to fragrant flower in five seconds. It does this only at dusk. The flowers twirl open, blasting their perfume into the air and attracting night-flying moths that pollinate them. A remarkable sight to behold.

In the temperate zones, temperature is clearly a product of time from hour to hour and month to month. I see more copperheads and corn snakes crossing roads at night during the summer. In early fall, when nights are cooler, they cross during the day. Daily and nightly temperatures dictate the activity levels of all snakes. Rainfall and moisture are obvious driving forces affecting the activity of countless animals and the local distributions of plants. Seasonal timing is the determinant of weather probabilities in a region. Whether it is night or day, hot or cold, wet or dry depends on time and season.

Winter Storm

A turkey vulture circles just above the loblolly pines that thrive on high ground in the swamp and tower far above the gray sweetgums and red maples, which will be waiting weeks for their own greenery. The pines are the sentinels. Their tops, moving like a cluster of upside-down whisk brooms propelled by an unseen hand, tell of a coming storm. Their backdrop is a silver-gray sky moving in layers that change from bright to dull as restless clouds shift over and under each other as they pass. The leafless hardwood saplings sway as the winter storm approaches.

The first rain droplets sound like an army of tiny insects moving among the crinkly brown leaves of autumn that have become winter's forest floor. Widely spaced droplets fall from the leaden sky, pockmarking the surface of the swamp. Within minutes the creek shimmers like a living canvas and the sound of falling raindrops echoes through the forest. A faint aroma fills the air, but not the petrichor of a summer rain. Is it the scent of ozone that drifts

At Salleyland any season can be appealing. A winter rain falling
in the swamp creates a tranquil scene. Photo by author.

in from unseen lightning announced by a distant rumbling? Is it the dank smell of rotting leaves disturbed by the gentle rain? Or does the fresh rain bring from the sky an olfactory sensation all its own?

The vulture no longer patrols from above. It either moved away, ahead of the storm, or is roosting atop one of the large white oaks on the forested hillside. Across the creek a raucous cacophony erupts from American crows. Stating their disapproval of a midday rain or sending a message to a barred owl that it needs to take its business elsewhere? Tiny brown swamp sparrows flit through the stand of switch cane bamboo that borders the creek, gradually disappearing as they take cover from the rain. Other small birds on the hillside chirp and flit among the trees with a sense of urgency. A breeze waxes and wanes as cooler air from west and north begins to intrude. A front is on the way.

I sit on the deck that overlooks creek and swamp, savoring the patter of rain on tin roof, the pockmarked surface of the water, the aromas of a rainy winter night at Salleyland. Without stirring I can take in the sights, sounds, and smells of tonight's nature show. I must move to engage taste and touch. Rousing myself, I walk outside, pick up a wet leaf, and touch my tongue to it. An altogether satisfying nocturnal adventure.

Springtime

As we hover around the spring equinox, get ready to experience the full joy of our natural heritage. Or as Mike puts it, "Nature, start your engines."

A trip to our woods and stream gave clear evidence of the transition to be seen over the next several weeks as fickle spring fluctuated between cold, warm, rainy, and windy. Though this particular day was on the cool side we found two small, sluggish snakes and a few lizards under flat boards we had set out for just that reason—to find snakes and lizards.

Most reptiles remain inactive during cool weather except on clear days when they can bask in the sun. Warm-blooded mammals and birds can be active during cold weather, and reproduction often starts in winter or early spring. Plus, Salleyland is a midway stopover region that migrating birds visit during their travels south in autumn and north in spring.

Later that day, Parker decided to check the wood duck boxes along the creek. Nailed to trees facing the water, these boxes have a large circular opening so that ducks can enter, lay eggs, and incubate them to hatching. A hinged door on the side can be opened for a look inside. The first two boxes led to high fives: one had ten wood duck eggs, the other had seventeen! The third box held its own surprises. When Parker opened the side door a gray squirrel jumped out and ran up the tree. After feeling around inside the box, Parker displayed the second surprise—two eyes-still-shut baby squirrels that he quickly returned to the box.

A warm spell was on the way and we often find rat snakes (which eat duck eggs) in the boxes. I wondered about the dynamics of the arms race between wood ducks and rat snakes. To get a science-based answer, I got in touch with Bobby Kennamer, a friend and colleague at SREL. Bobby has conducted the most impressive long-term ecological studies on rat snakes and wood ducks ever published in the scientific literature. He has been capturing wood ducks for more than thirty years and has counted nearly forty-five thousand eggs.

According to Bobby, usually a wood duck hen lays an egg a day, for around twelve to fourteen days. He noted that the box with seventeen eggs was "almost certainly the work of more than one female." The interloper's eggs will be incubated unknowingly by the first occupant of the nest. Egg incubation does not begin until a female lays almost all of her eggs, at which point she sits on the eggs at night. Bobby says that "when the clutch is complete, full incubation is initiated during both day and night," with the female taking morning and evening feeding recesses. The male stays nearby, perhaps as a sentinel but also for retaining a pair bond with the female should renesting become an option.

Once rat snakes enter the springtime scene, they patrol woods, swamps, and streams searching for open tree cavities that might have nesting birds or squirrels. A duck box with a large hole is a well-defined lure for a big rat snake, which can eat as many as ten duck eggs in one sitting. When a snake enters the box, the hen will usually pass him at the front door as she makes her escape and flies away. I have yet to see this at Salleyland, but a big rat snake will occasionally corner and kill the hen herself by constricting her around the neck. This is a fool's errand for a rat snake because a wood duck is too large to swallow, and a dead wood duck will never be able to provide more eggs for hungry rat snakes. The eggs are the real target, and the snake may stay in the nest box for several days while it digests them. Once the female wood duck figures out that a rat snake has invaded her nest, even though there may still be uneaten eggs in the box, she will often abandon the nest and set about laying eggs elsewhere.

The springtime race is underway, with squirrels and ducks in the starting lineup. Then, as warm weather sets in, the snakes will be out, looking for their first meal. Nature's racetrack is longer than any of NASCAR's and has far more participants. Spectators can marvel for many weeks as spring calls forth a dazzling array of predators and prey as well as scavengers that thrive only on the dead.

A Salleyland Summer

A summer at Salleyland is like a summer anywhere else in the South. Most summers are different from each other, yet few are unusual. To paraphrase Justin Congdon, an unusual summer is a summer that is like a previous one. Turns out virtually none of our summers are alike. Expect heat and humidity and on many days you will not be wrong. But in some years temperatures never reach one hundred degrees; in others, we all wonder when the hundred-degree days will end. No one expects summer to be over by Labor Day. That expectation is met every year. Nonetheless much of a Salleyland summer leaves fine memories.

The morning was cool and pleasant for August when Nick, Keith, and I pushed off from shore. Most summer mornings are like that and the weather stays tolerable at least until noon. Widely spaced, white, fluffy clouds taxied around and in front of the sun, subtly shifting the cerulean sky from pale to darker. We looked over the side of our Jon boat (what I called a flat-bottomed boat growing up) into the aptly named blackwater creek. If you put creek water in a glass, you will find it clear as crystal or perhaps like the weakest iced tea you'll ever find. The blackwater imagery comes from peering through transparent water to a bottom of dark mud, rich in tannins and decomposing vegetation.

We drifted downstream, following the open water that snaked through the smartweed that appeared to be an impenetrable aquatic pasture surrounding us. Roots that looked like they would stop our progress were readily dislodged when we veered too far left or right. The swipe of a paddle uprooted whole plants and our progress was not slowed. At a few places, we welcomed the appearance of another dominant aquatic plant of the entire stream system—American bur-reed. This close relative of the common cattails we had just passed growing alongshore is an indicator of faster moving open water in the stream in sections unclogged by smartweed. Leaves of the bur-reed undulate underwater like long, green straps above a sandy bottom where mud has been swept away by the current. The late summer's day was ideal for a downstream boat trip. It was about to get even better.

Keith and I were doing the paddling, which required little effort, while Nick perched on the bow looking for insects, lizards, and snakes on the vegetation. He pointed out a bright green anole as it scampered up a tulip poplar growing along shore. The lizard did a couple of pushups and extended its strawberry red dewlap as it looked down on us from the lowest limb. As our little craft drifted beneath him he continued his combative display until he was confident he had driven us away.

We landed the boat at an area we call the Beach. Originally we thought this would be the site for the cabin so most of the shrubby vegetation had been cleared away right down to the water's edge. We pulled the boat up on shore. We planned to walk back to the cabin and leave the boat for a later trip upstream. Nick was leading the way as we walked up toward SNAP Road. I looked ahead about thirty feet and felt like I had just seen three bars show up on a slot machine. But these bars were a natural jackpot. They were the black chevrons contrasted against the light gray body of an enormous canebrake rattlesnake.

We walked over to the snake, which had moved into some low vegetation near the base of a large sweetgum tree. It watched warily, keeping its face toward us and its body angled toward a large hole beneath the tree's roots. Standing six feet away, we could see the gray head, lighter colored chin, and brown wash behind the vertical-pupiled eyes. Having assessed its odds against three primates totaling more than a hundred times its own weight, the snake moved backward until its body was alongside the underground retreat, gave one click of a long string of rattles, and disappeared.

We first found her on August 9. She was in the entrance to the hole or a few feet out in the vegetation at least nine more times over the next month when we wanted to show her to visitors. She had apparently become accustomed to us, for her retreats when we approached were more languid, unhurried. Her five babies were born on Labor Day. Mike and Parker found them and came to get the rest of us. Canebrake rattlesnakes display parental care to the extent that the newborn stay around the mother for several days, until they shed their skin for the first time. I was alone a week later when I went to the tree hole, found five small snakeskins, and checked in the burrow with a flashlight. Nobody was home or anywhere to be seen. Summer was still with us when we said goodbye to the mother rattlesnake and her babies. A good summer it had been.

Changes of Autumn

On the front porch of the cabin I catch an allusion to the changes autumn brings as I watch a green anole turn brown before my eyes. The oak, sweetgum, and maple trees have taken weeks to make the color shift, many still a work in progress. I move to the back porch overlooking the stream to watch scattered fast-moving white clouds against a pale blue sky. I listen to the wind rustling the switch cane, watch it swaying plume grass along the banks. As the wind picks up, the sound of creaking trees becomes more noticeable. Red, yellow, and brown leaves fall like snowflakes heralding a winter storm. Some land in the water and drift upstream like tiny sailboats against the slow current.

A burst of wind launches white oak acorns that land with authority on the tin roof, each providing its own attention-getting report. Falling temperatures prompt me to put on my denim jacket. In the firepit, the wood from last night's fire still smolders, bringing the familiar smell of a dead campfire long past flames. A can of smoked oysters, some saltine crackers, and a Dr Pepper qualify as healthy eating on a fishing boat, in a deer stand, or at a cabin in the woods. During a momentary lull in the wind, I see clear reflections in the pool below the wooden footbridge, the tops of barren water tupelo trees in the swamp, their leaves already part of autumn's natural carpet. Only the pine trees on the high ground in the swamp are green, swaying with the wind and, immune to autumn's whims, with no intention of turning brown like anoles or other trees.

Turning my gaze from the swamp to the forest, I visualize the coming changes. Soon the American holly trees will reign as the only evergreen hardwoods on the hillside alongside larger, barren oaks, sweetgums, and red maples. The flowering dogwood, also deciduous, greets autumn with dignity. If trees could muse, some might strive to be like the dogwood. It never challenges the mighty oaks or pines in stature, living beneath them in relative obscurity. Yet the dogwood is hailed for its spectacular floral displays in spring and is equally appreciated in the fall as its emerald, ruby red, and burgundy leaves hold on through the last cold, dark, wet, and windy days of winter, finally drifting to the ground to lie atop the dull brown leaves of oak and copper-colored needles of pine.

Any Time Is a Good Time

During any season, time of day is vital in the search for most animals. Plants are more accommodating because they stay in the same place day and night, although they don't all bloom at the same time. Likewise, the windows of opportunity for discovering many animals open and close by the clock. The transitions from day to night and back are critical for determining the probabilities of a sighting for some species. And the ideal time of day or night shifts in response to the seasons, the weather, and sometimes factors known only to the organisms themselves.

A crepuscular animal is one whose most active periods center around dusk or dawn. Sitting on the open deck at the cabin, I hear the first and last chirrs of gray squirrels just before the sun rises and as it sets. I assume they are talking to each other and not to me, although maybe about me. Reptiles, amphibians, and mammals are often sighted in summer during the hour or so after sunset (the so-called golden hour). Rain changes the odds entirely. You are less likely to see snakes and mammals and more likely to see frogs and salamanders. Herpetologists have endless debates about the best times and conditions to road cruise for snakes. Some claim a peak in activity occurs during the period before sunrise (the platinum hour).

My experience has been that successful road cruising for snakes or other animals is like your odds in a casino. Season and time of day, temperature and humidity, reproductive stage and sex of the individual, and a host of other factors all play a role. Arriving in your vehicle at the same moment an animal is crossing the road is like pulling the slot machine lever. Sometimes you hit the jackpot. Sometimes you go home broke.

Learning the day/night behavior of an animal of interest can be a challenge. At Salleyland we have documented finding more than five hundred green anoles, in every season, but we have never seen one out and about at night. Categorizing animals as to their propensity for diurnal or nocturnal behavior makes us aware of how different one species can be from another and how different a particular species can be from one time to the next.

We have found ten kinds of frogs at Salleyland, and the best way to describe when they call is that any of them might call at any time of day, although some have tendencies for night or day only. Southern toads, narrow-mouthed toads, and green treefrogs take the night shift unless daytime rains in warm weather are on the docket. Cricket frogs show up for work during the day but will take the night shift as well. Bronze frogs, gray treefrogs, squirrel treefrogs, and spring peepers are on the clock 24-7, but the large choruses are at night or after heavy rains. Leopard frogs and bullfrogs are mostly nighttime croakers, but a daytime chuckle or boom is not considered unusual.

Don't fret about the variability and unpredictability of any particular animal's behavior. They know what they are doing. And they are not doing it for us. Just enjoy those times when you pull the handle and hit the jackpot.

Know Your Habitats

Turned out to be a beautiful day and not too hot—perfect for visiting a variety of habitats. We walked into the swamp, across the field, and through the woods. Patricia West and David Hothem found the first live box turtle at Salleyland as it plodded through oak and hickory leaves, going about its business. Parker caught slimy salamanders, southern toads, fence lizards, and we saw a basking slider turtle at Green Pond. Habitat diversity makes a difference.

SALLEYLAND FIELD NOTES, JUNE 23, 2013

HABITAT DIVERSITY BEGETS SPECIES DIVERSITY. SOME ANIMALS AND plants are generalists, which is a polite way of saying they have no discriminating tastes compared to the specialists. Slider turtles are the consummate generalists in the world of herpetology. They are now considered to be an invasive species in dozens of countries and on every continent except the one that is always the exception—Antarctica. They may even end up there if certain global warming models are correct. They can live and thrive almost anywhere with freshwater habitats around. Some consider them more cosmopolitan, more worldly, than most other vertebrate species in the world, although Norway rats are even more pervasive. Specialists are more provincial, remaining faithful to their roots. Mud salamanders fit the bill as habitat specialists. Salleyland's soon-to-be-revealed high biodiversity, of reptiles and amphibians as well as many other groups of plants and animals, is a consequence of its four distinct habitats, each home to specialists not found in any of the others.

Anyone who thrives on being outdoors should try viewing any new habitat, whether public park or private land, as a mosaic to be categorized into its component natural parts. Any habitat can be partitioned into microhabitats for those who wish to catalog on a finer scale. A southwestern desert may have open areas amid clumps of cacti and mesquite trees partitioning the scene into discrete living quarters or foraging sites for diverse species. A mountain habitat in the Appalachians can be partitioned into rocky slopes, clear streams, and thick banks of rhododendrons, each providing homes for a different array of native species. Even a backyard can offer its own filing system of open grass, shrubs, and trees. Each will be of some value to animals that thrive on one or another for special needs. Check your surroundings when out and about and set up your own scheme for categorizing and describing the habitats and microhabitats you find.

The Swamp

One reason Salleyland could be purchased for less than most of the land within thirty miles in any direction was because a big chunk of it was "worthless swampland." To farm it would require draining it, and its proximity to a creek that frequently floods would make occasional crop losses a

Myriad plants and animals inhabit the Salleyland sphagnum swamp, a distinctive ecosystem. Photo by Stephen Bennett.

certainty. Recreational horseback riders prefer solid ground, as do hunters of deer, squirrel, and turkey. But value is in the eye of the beholder. To a herpetologist, several acres of a giant natural sponge known as sphagnum moss are a treasure trove. The area provides ideal habitat for a variety of amphibians less likely to be found in other areas. Eventually we would identify mud salamanders, Chamberlain's dwarf salamanders, two- and three-lined salamanders, and the rare many-lined salamanders as inhabitants of the Salleyland sphagnum swamp. Few of them wander far from its margins.

Sphagnum is a generic term encompassing more than three hundred species of mosses worldwide. Dead and decaying sphagnum is often a basic component of peat moss harvested for fuel in some parts of the world. In horticulture, sphagnum is a primary ingredient in certain potting soils. Sphagnum's ability to retain water is remarkable. During short periods of drought, the Salleyland sphagnum swamp becomes yellowish brown as the surface water recedes and plants appear to shrivel. With the first rain the swamp rejuvenates overnight into a lush emerald carpet.

The bog-like sphagnum swamp is more acidic than other bodies of water in the vicinity because of the underlying decay in low-oxygen waters. It is of untold value to small salamanders. During field trips we often find two dozen or more salamanders under coverboards we have set out for the sole purpose of finding animals. The surface area of the boards is a minuscule portion of the total surface area of the swamp. Basic extrapolation would suggest that total salamander numbers in the swamp are extraordinarily high. Coverboards do not attract salamanders. They are found in proportional numbers under any natural cover, including rotting logs, decaying leaves, even the sphagnum itself. Without question, hundreds if not thousands or possibly tens of thousands of larval and adult salamanders live in the few acres comprising the swamp.

Walking through the swamp during the growing season conjures up an almost tropical ambiance. Tall tupelo gum trees bring deep shade, with smaller trees such as red bay, sweet bay magnolias, and red maples filling in gaps where sunshine might slip through. Waist-high cinnamon ferns and tall royal ferns could be textbook images of the Late Carboniferous geological period. Greenbrier vines twist and twine up, down, and sideways, ever ready to make you pay attention to their thorns. Shelf mushrooms adorn most trees. The swamp holds many mysteries and provides constant entertainment. Viewed through the right eyes, the Salleyland sphagnum swamp is not worthless after all.

The Sands

We didn't own the field at first and wouldn't still if Susan Lane and Keith had not taken a liking to what we were doing and elected to buy 35 acres of mostly sandhill habitat to add to Salleyland. Sandhills and their distinctive flora and fauna are part of a southeastern ecological community of rolling sands marking the boundary between the Coastal Plain and the Piedmont. The ocean that once covered the region is no longer in sight, having receded southeasterly a hundred miles over the past several million years. The majestic forests that once covered 90 million acres of the longleaf pine–sandhill ecosystem from Virginia to Texas are now represented only by scattered remnants (less than 5 percent of what greeted the first European colonists, some reports suggest). Our sandhill was included in the excessive timbering, probably more than a century ago.

We set about on an opposite course by planting sixteen thousand longleaf pine seedlings. Some of the trees have sunk their deep taproots and are now taller than any of us. Programs by the nonprofit Longleaf Alliance and the federal Natural Resource Conservation Service aided our efforts to return the habitat to its pretimbering distinctiveness. Our contribution is tiny. But if everyone with sandhill property made a similar effort, we might soon return to a semblance of what was once a thriving, diverse, and majestic ecosystem.

The sands are so deep and uniform that when Stewart the Dog died, Keith and Nick buried him at the top of the ridge without ever hitting a root. The prairie-like scene with low vegetative ground cover and thousands of small longleaf pines is surprisingly diverse zoologically. Ground skinks, glass lizards, and scarlet snakes are common inhabitants of sandhills, and we have found them all. Each coachwhip snake, another tenant of sandhill habitat, has been a treasure to find, especially when it is the first one many visitors have ever seen. Other snakes have made cameo appearances—canebrake rattlesnakes and eastern hognose snakes at the edge fronting the swamp margin. The single adult pine snake was headed toward the field from across the road. A sandy hillside dotted with burrows from oldfield mice ensures the availability of prey for mammal-eating predators and underground refuges for smaller sandhill creatures.

Our beehives are on the western edge of the field, shielded from the brutal afternoon suns of summer by a copse of water oak trees lining the top edge of the sandhill. The bees thrive with the warmth of a rising sun, access to water in the swamp, and myriad flowering native plants from which to gather nectar and pollen. Tupelo honey is a prize among beekeepers, and our bees know where to find blooms in the tops of the tallest trees in the swamp. The display of autumn flowers abloom in the field creates a colorful collage accompanied by an endless array of wasps, bumblebees, butterflies, and other native insects.

The Woods

A mean-spirited botanist might refer to our woods as being "second-growth forest, at best, maybe third or fourth." As pre-nineteenth-century temperate zone forests are exceedingly rare anywhere in the world, and becoming rarer each year, when hearing such a disagreeable remark, one response is to turn palms up, raise your shoulders and say, "And your point would be?" Another response might be, "Yes, but it is my forest, and the trees continue to grow every year." Actually, I've only heard this critical observation once and will not hear it again from the same person. My suggested responses are available to any private landowner owning a small piece of earth covered by trees.

Most visitors to our woods, including me, love walking through the hillside forest beneath the high canopy of mockernut hickory, sweetgums, and a variety of oaks, including red, scarlet, and white. Apparently the early clearcutting loggers didn't get them all, as a few are two to three feet in diameter. On one special patch I can show a visitor an example of longleaf, loblolly, and shortleaf pine within a tree's length of each other. We entertain kids by giving them a measuring tape and sending them up the forested hillside to see who can find the tree with the greatest DBH (diameter breast high) as botanists call it.

One appeal of a walk in the Salleyland woods is the easily navigable understory of widely spaced flowering dogwoods, sparkleberry, and small American holly trees. We have created paths through the woods, but the open understory with no impeding blackberry bushes, greenbrier vines, or doghobble invites exploration in any direction. Being hostages of human nature, most folks follow the path where the last person walked. On warm days, temperatures are usually a few degrees lower in the woods than in the field; humidity is lower than in the swamp. A summer rainstorm announcing its approach with a darkening cloud followed by the rapid pummeling of high leaves encourages visitors to take cover or stand at the base of a big oak or hickory. If lightning is in the offing—head for the cabin. I have walked the woods of Salleyland in every season and every weather. I have heard the patter of sleet on a ground covering of fallen leaves and strained to hear the near silent fall of snow as the brown-leaved ground whitened. I consider our woods as the rebirth of a virgin forest.

The Stream

Goodland Creek is a tributary to the South Fork, which merges with the North Fork near Branchville, South Carolina, to form the Edisto River, which in turn runs into the Atlantic Ocean at Edisto Island between Charleston and Hilton Head. The system of undammed, meandering streams, with ox-bow lakes typical of Coastal Plain rivers offers a navigable waterway from Salleyland to the ocean. But we are content to paddle canoe, kayak, and Jon boat north to south along the half mile bordered by our own property.

Like all habitats in the Southeast, the stream's character changes with the seasons. Winter brings too-cold-for-swimming waters. In the spring-time American bur-reed waves its green ribbons down the center of the fast-flowing stream. The thick growth of smartweed will not begin to choke the stream from the margins until summer is on the scene. Keeping a stream path open requires weekly boat trips as summer progresses. Waiting a month or more makes finding the main downstream channel difficult. Smartweed wants to fill the stream. Upstream from the cabin is different. Both sides have less floodplain and are more shaded by the shoreline trees. The stream is open year-round. Upstream from the cabin, the water appears to flow at a discernible rate. Downstream seems more like sluggish backwater. Both ends are actually flowing at the same rate of gallons per minute, but the stream broadens as it moves south, creating flooded pools and giving the appearance of moving more slowly. When the aquatic vegetation diminishes in autumn, the clear stream of winter and spring reappears.

Our inventories of stream fauna and flora have come from curious botanists, surveys of stream invertebrates by the South Carolina Department of Natural Resources (DNR), and our own sampling of fish and herps. Two conspicuous stream plants, green arrow arum with its enormous emergent leaves and the unrelated broadleaf arrowhead, margin the shallow shorelines in many areas. Though the two plants look alike, they differ structurally and when in flower. Arrow arum has inedible flowers that look like small ears of corn and are pollinated by a type of small fly. Broadleaf arrowhead has pretty white flowers. It is sometimes called duck potato because its tubers growing in the mud can be eaten if properly prepared. Sounds to me like a meal of last resort or one you partake of so you can casually mention it at a cocktail party. Among my favorite stream plants are turtle heads with their beautiful white flowers suffused with pink. They are uncommon and finding them when they are blooming in late summer is a treat. Remembering where you saw one the year before is important. American snowbell, a small deciduous tree, is another eye-catching streamside prize. Its tiny white flowers hang like bells along its branches in spring and early summer.

South Carolina DNR entomologist David Eargle gets full credit for being the first to point out the diversity of Goodland Creek invertebrates. Thus far he has identified more than one hundred species, which represents only a small percentage of the total. When David came in July to take the first samples, Parker, Nick, and I served as his assistants. For about an hour, we used dip nets and a small seine to sample silty areas in the creek near the cabin, capturing freshwater shrimp, clams, chironomid fly larvae, dragonfly and damselfly larvae, and a variety of other taxonomic orders of insects. We then walked upstream along a woodland path and found a well-marked deer trail that we followed to the creek, ending up in a narrow (twelve feet wide), fast-moving part of the stream with perfectly clear water and sandy bottom. Here we found lots of aquatic larvae of caddisflies, more odonates, and a stonefly, all signs of a healthy stream. David came again the following February and added freshwater mussels and fingernail clams to the list of inhabitants.

The stream and its floodplain margins are home to numerous kinds of fishes and herps. None of the reptiles are restricted to the aquatic habitat per se, as all will venture onto land. And many of the smaller fish species are found in swamp pools after flooding. Goodland Creek is the environmental heart for many life-forms. Some are fully dependent on the stream. Others would persist, but the supplementary resources of an aquatic ecosystem make a greater abundance more likely.

A Landscape Mystery

As with any area with landscape diversity, the major habitats of Salleyland can be partitioned into microhabitats, which can be reduced to components on an even finer scale. For example, a suburban backyard might be partitioned into two definable habitats: open lawn and bordering shrubs. If moles have made tunnels across parts of the lawn, these become a microhabitat distinct from the undisturbed grass. Open and active mole tunnels are a further partitioning of microhabitats as would be the centipede grass section compared to the patch of zoysia. Within the shrubs, areas covered by ivy or Virginia creeper might be microhabitats compared to other areas of bare soil. Presumably, the narrowing of environmental function of a habitat might be called nanohabitats, picohabitats, all the way down to yoctohabitats or smaller. To life-forms as small as bacteria, whether one is under a blade of grass or an inch away in open sunlight can make a life-or-death difference.

At Salleyland we have identified several microhabitats distinctive enough to be given names. Coming through the woods down the hill from the top ridge, we come to a carved-out gulley about twenty feet deep and the same width. A few feet away is a similar landform with the same dimensions. Both little valleys with their dirt and clay walls travel for about a hundred feet before they converge into a single corridor that soon merges into the surrounding woods. We call it the Blowout because when we first discovered the big hole in the woods it looked like the soil had been blown away by a major explosion. I fantasized. Could it be the product of a long-forgotten dynamite charge set decades ago? Did a tiny asteroid pick that spot to land? Was it a natural geological feature of some sort?

I like to take geologists, agriculturists, and visitors with a land management or forest resources background to the Blowout to see what they think created it. I have enjoyed the mix of conflicting guesses, hypotheses, and downright declarations almost as much as I would an unequivocally correct answer. Some visitors have authoritatively declared that the Blowout is a result of land erosion where soil had been removed by humans early in the previous century. None has given a convincing explanation for why anyone would come into the woods and dig up a bunch of dirt in a rural area before earthmoving equipment was common. And where did the dirt go?

Some ecologically minded visitors have suggested that the Blowout represents stream channel remnants of runoff from a long-ago spring or seep that surfaced on the hillside and eventually dried up. Others have stated that it was related in some way to agricultural activities associated with draining the flat terrain at the top of the hill. Or, perhaps, long ago, when the woods were probably clear-cut, the hillside itself was farmed. Due to the slope, it was necessary to terrace the planting area, and indeed several flat, steplike rows the width of a roadbed parallel the stream far below. But no one has articulated to my satisfaction how the processes involved would have created two small valleys reminiscent of ancient tributaries into a single stream in the middle of the woods. A meteor strike has not been mentioned by anyone yet, but I'm waiting.

Identifying microhabitats can lead to a search for answers to landscape mysteries. I have not exhausted attempts to find out the true origin of the Blowout. I will be asking more visitors for their opinions. If I could find near-century-old aerial photographs, they might disclose what the terrain looked like before and after. Trying to resolve the origin of a deep gully in an otherwise uniform landscape in a forest has turned out to be more fascinating and far more entertaining than I thought. Wherever your own outdoor pursuits take you, define some of the microhabitats and determine why they are different from their surroundings.

The Early Inhabitants

Salleyland's sands, swamps, and forests have been mostly unchanged by natural forces for centuries. No doubt the stream channels shifted over time with floods and droughts, but the hillside slope stayed at about the same angle. The dominant forest covering the landscape would have changed in character periodically following ancient lightning fires but always eventually returning to the oak-hickory climax on the hillside and longleaf pine ecosystem on the sandhills. Only when land-shaping agriculture began in the region two centuries ago did the habitat take on its current environmental demeanor. But before European colonization, the area now called Salleyland had other residents who also left evidence of their existence—Native Americans.

A piece in the historical puzzle of any land area is who was there before you arrived. Will Dillman found the first piece to our puzzle in 2017. We had walked more than two miles that day looking for herps and were standing in an open sandy area when Will picked up a gray pottery shard about the shape and thickness of a matchbook. A small rock I thought. Then we all looked closer. On the outer side of the slightly concave object was a clear crisscrossed indentation where a small vine had been pressed into wet clay long ago. Decorative, corded pottery! I gave the shard to Rooney Floyd, a friend who did volunteer work with Chris Moore, an archaeologist at the University of South Carolina. Chris and Rooney confirmed the pottery was authentic. Three months later we assembled at the cabin to take a look at the area and assess the significance of what was unequivocally a human artifact.

We settled on the back porch with coffee as Chris and Rooney began their strategic planning.

The first step was to examine a two-foot-by-two-foot LiDAR photograph to select sites for preliminary shovel tests. Depending on which archaeologist or geologist you talk to LiDAR stands for "light detection and ranging" or "laser imaging, detection, and ranging." The image lying on the table was an aerial view of Salleyland taken with laser technology, which measures the ground surface of the area without being confounded by tree cover. Differences of only a foot or so in soil elevation could be detected on the LiDAR image. To Chris and Rooney, the LiDAR revealed small islands in the swamp and terraces on the hillside where early travelers a millennium earlier might have camped. I imagined myself in a scene from *Raiders of the Lost Ark* and wished I had Harrison Ford's hat.

An hour later we were at the first preliminary shovel site. The person doing the digging threw sand, clay, and dirt into a quarter-inch hardware cloth frame that the other held as a filter, leaving any larger objects on top. In the swamp, on an island detected with LiDAR, we found a fire-cracked rock about a foot beneath the surface (28 cm by their precise measurement). According to Chris, Native Americans would heat rocks to drop into a clay pot of water to warm it up or, before clay pottery was available, into an animal skin bag.

In one spot we reached a layer of fine yellow sand that went down for several inches until a thin horizon of dark soil appeared. Chris said that layer probably represented an ancient forest fire, leaving a strip of dark gray ash. Below, the soil became sandy again, continuing vertically back into time. The eureka moment came when a distinctive blue-tinted, translucent flake with serrated edges appeared in the filter frame. Chris picked it up and, hand outstretched, held it in front of me. He said it was unquestionably a piece of flint "shaped by the hand of man" hundreds or possibly thousands of years ago. That was an exciting find: confirmation that humans had experienced the sands, swamps, and forests of Salleyland long before my ancestors had experienced America.

Get Off the Beaten Path

I absolutely loved staying here this weekend and finding dozens of bird species, including eastern bluebirds, northern parula warblers, Carolina chickadees, red-shouldered hawks, and a barred owl. I even heard a hooded warbler! A black rat snake full of duck eggs it had eaten was in one box and a female duck sitting on a dozen eggs was in another. We found mud salamanders, and Parker stepped on a big fat cottonmouth at the beaver dam. I love herping with Parker. It's like heaven with the wildlife, scenery, and parulas calling!

MATTHEW McDONALD, SALLEYLAND GUEST LOG, MARCH 19, 2016

IN ECOLOGY, ANY TAXONOMIC FIELD HAS ITS COLLECTING TECHNIQUES for documenting what is present in a region, specific locality, or type of habitat. Samples for museums and research laboratories must not only be found but also collected or photographed. Blood samples or tissue for DNA analysis may be needed. Scientific papers in ecological journals typically have a materials and methods section in which detailed descriptions of techniques used to collect the plants or animals are given. In taxonomically oriented journals such as *Herpetological Review*, some of the articles describe innovative methods of finding certain organisms. Numerous wildlife books dedicate a section or chapter to methods for locating and capturing target species.

Trying to outsmart wildlife, especially clandestine animals that are experts at concealing themselves, can be a fun, challenging exercise. Developing techniques to document the presence of animals and to observe or catch them can become a goal in itself. Using different field techniques broadens our perspective about what wildlife might be in our midst. For a certainty any natural or even agriculturally developed rural habitats that are not

Large rat snakes, common visitors to duck boxes in the spring, can eat
as many as ten duck eggs at one time. Photo by Mike Gibbons.

megafarms and are near water will likely have more native wildlife inhabitants than you imagine. We found unexpectedly high diversity at Salleyland. Many more species of mammals, reptiles, amphibians, and fishes revealed themselves over time than I had anticipated.

I intentionally omitted birds, invertebrates, and plants from the list of species with unforeseen high numbers. Professional ornithologists, even just plain old amateur bird-watchers, can run up a respectable bird list in short order from both sights and sounds. I can recognize the common ones, if they are big enough or loud enough. I admire the identification skills of bird people. My technique for adding birds to my faunal list is to be sure a bird-watcher is by my side. As for invertebrates, especially insects and spiders, who knows what to expect if you're not an entomologist or arachnologist? Likewise, with plants. Who in the world can guess how many grasses, sedges, or mosses might cover the landscape of any given area unless these groups are their specialty?

Not knowing what you might discover adds to the mystique of any habitat by turning the first visit into an exploratory adventure. Subsequent visits

Parker holds on to a tree as a nesting female wood duck leaves the box. Wood ducks are the most common species of waterfowl at Salleyland. Photo by Mike Gibbons.

will lead to an ever-growing list of species, which will add to your knowledge and your enjoyment.

Take a Stroll

One of the surest ways to find plants and animals is by taking a walk through woods, field, or swamp. If water is involved, walk along the stream bank or get in a canoe. If birds or dragonflies are the organisms of interest, use binoculars. The common denominator is to see what you can find by chance encounter.

Botanists lead a simple life when it comes to studying species of interest. If they find a tree that holds some kind of fascination for them, it will be in the same spot in every season. Finding it again is easy. Refinding flowers adds a temporal dimension, because they are seasonal. The precise location of the plant itself may have to be marked in some way for a return trip. Annuals complicate the issue as they may not be in the exact spot the following year. But even they will probably be in the same general area. Overall, botanists have an easy time finding their quarry. I'm not aware of any plant that will run away or try to hide.

Strolling is the first step in determining what species of animals inhabit a given land area, whether a backyard, larger acreage of private land, state park, wildlife refuge, or national forest. Checking out habitats and micro-habitats will provide the first clues of what species might be present—and sometimes provide clear evidence of their presence. Our first discoveries of numerous species were those we encountered during walks around the property with no particular goal in mind.

Deer are not uncommon in the Southeast like they once were, as recently as a half century ago in some areas. I spent my childhood roaming the woods and swamps of Alabama and Louisiana. I did not see my first wild deer until I was fifteen. Deer are a staple of the mammal fauna of Salleyland, confirmed by observations and many wildlife camera records, but I well recall (with the help of my field notes) the first one I saw there. Carolyn and I were taking Maddux the Dog for a walk off-leash in the woods. Maddux is a hefty, powerful boxer, with a coat brown on back and sides and white on the belly, not dissimilar to a white-tailed deer. According to my notes, "We had put an orange ribbon on Maddux so that he would not look too much like a deer since it is still hunting season. Of course, some South Carolina hunters might not wonder why a doe would be sporting orange ribbon until after they brought it down and discovered it not only had no antlers, but no hooves. Nonetheless, we would be able to tell Mike that we had *tried* to keep him safe." Maddux does not consider himself as an outdoor dog and usually keeps his white feet clean to assure access to the nearest couch. But he was clearly enjoying this romp through the wood.

As we entered the stand of loblolly pine along the top ridge above where the cabin was being built, Maddux ambled confidently toward a clump of sparkleberry and beautyberry bushes growing alongside a fallen pine tree. I saw him stop, ears up. Out of the greenery a deer bolted. Carolyn and I stopped cold, with the rush of adrenaline you get when startled. The deer easily cleared the horizontal tree trunk and was gracefully threading its way through the open areas between trees in the stand. The sparse ground vegetation afforded a perfect view of its bounding leaps and white tail flag waving goodbye.

Maddux took off after it like a racehorse. I figured Mike's dog was gone and probably would be unable to find his way back from the next county after the deer had shown the dog that it was not only faster than a racehorse but could run longer distances. Nonetheless, in desperation I gave a sharp two-fingered whistle and yelled, "Maddux. Stop!" To our surprise, he did. Only fifty yards from us. Carolyn, the dog, and I watched the deer disappear into the woods. Maddux then turned and trotted back to us. The look in his eye seemed to say, "I ran it away. My work here is done. I know you're proud." I told him he was a good dog.

The stroll through the woods demonstrated the tiered approach to keeping a listing of confirmed wildlife. I already knew deer were there based on numerous observations of hoof prints and occasional droppings. But in-person confirmation is like removing the asterisk from a sports record. I gave Maddux credit for the deer sighting and considered the day's stroll to have been a good walk unspoiled.

Set a Target

Aimless wandering through the woods rewards with wildlife surprises. Targeting a species and finding it rewards with a sense of accomplishment. Having an objective can add focus to a field trip, and accomplishing that objective brings great satisfaction. Our documentation of the rough green snake at Salleyland fulfilled hopes beyond all expectations.

Our first hint that rough green snakes were on the property came on an early spring afternoon. Nick Tindall, whom we referred to as Nick the

Builder to avoid confusion with Nick the Grandson, was clearing SNAP Road to get to the cabin site. He said he had run over and killed a snake with his Bobcat, a compact tractor. He was apologetic. I knew it was an accident. He adhered to my strict instructions not to intentionally harm any wildlife, especially snakes, while he was building the cabin. His description of a green snake that had turned blue when he looked at it a couple of hours later gave no doubt as to what it was. A bright green snake with a pale-yellow belly is not to be confused with any other native snake in the region. The green color is a combination of yellow pigment overlying structural arrangements of cells that reflect blue. When a green snake dies, the yellow pigment ceases to function and only the blue is apparent. Rough green snakes are ubiquitous throughout their southeastern geographic range, so I added it to our list of snakes. Nonetheless, I always have reservations when I have not seen the animal myself. I was looking forward to in-hand documentation.

Seven months later, I found a shed skin along the shore of the stream. A shed skin is as good as the snake itself as far as counting the configuration of scales on the head and body. It keyed out to be a rough green snake, but the fact we had not yet caught one nagged at me. Then came the night in May, a year and two months after Nick the Builder's report of a green snake that turned blue.

Mike, Parker, and I were spending the night at the cabin when I suggested we go looking for green snakes in trees above the creek at night. This is one of the classic techniques for finding them. Looking for these masters of camouflage during the day generally means getting fooled by green vines and foliage. I have seen someone point out a green snake resting in a tree to someone else standing only five feet away. The snake might as well have been invisible. But at night, when a green snake is sleeping in vegetation high above the ground, a flashlight reveals a bright yellow belly amid the surrounding green.

An hour before midnight, we eased the canoe into the water to drift downstream. Mike and I sat in the back while Parker sat astride the bow, our flashlights illuminating the overhanging limbs of alder, water tupelo, and sweetgum trees. We had floated no more than a hundred feet when Mike said, "There's one." It was draped over a tangle of greenbrier vines, its green back looking like another vine but its brilliant underside shining beaconlike in the glare of three flashlights.

I spoke next. "Parker sit down till we get over to it. It's not going anywhere." I did not bother to tell him how many times I have ended up in the water because someone had treated a canoe or Jon boat like they were walking through their living room.

In ten minutes we had found our quarry and Parker had it in hand, the first rough green snake he had ever seen in the wild. He sat on the end of the canoe and examined it, his excitement evident. When we got back to the canoe landing, we high-fived our successful venture. I gave silent thanks that I would not have an entry in my field notes about a capsized canoe.

The most unusual part of that evening's adventure? It was too easy. Finding green snakes at night can be effective. But some stream trips last an hour or more before the first one is seen. Sometimes we don't find one at all, which is disappointing but tempts one to try again.

Set Out Coverboards

Sam found and caught the first individual of the tenth species of snake (and thirty-fifth reptile or amphibian) to be documented at Salleyland, in part because of misidentification. Jennifer Anne, Sam, and I had walked to an open grassy area with several wild plum trees, surrounded by oak-hickory woods. We call the place the Old Homesite, not because we found old bricks or boards, but because it is a distinct microhabitat where a dwelling might have once stood. Earlier in the year we had put half a dozen pieces of discarded tin roofing on the ground.

We turned over the first few coverboards to see if any animals were under them and found a couple of large black beetles that were notable for being purple on the edges. When Sam turned over the next tin sheet, he stared for a moment then reached down and grabbed what he took to be a worm. When they were young, before they could make their own identifications, all of the children knew not to pick up a snake unless I had said it was okay. But a worm? No problem. Except Sam and I both realized at the same time that he held a small brown snake—a southeastern crowned snake.

I knew Salleyland was within the geographic range of these small serpents and had them on our list of possibles. But this was the first one we had seen. Crowned snakes are pretty little creatures with a glossy dark tan body and a black nose and head. Crowned snakes never bite people, and even if they tried, their mouths are too small to get a grip. Despite their docile nature and inoffensive appearance, they are formidable predators on what seems like improbable prey—venomous centipedes. An exciting find for the day, soon to be reported by Sam to Nick and Parker.

Without question, coverboards are the most effective and efficient technique for finding certain kinds of animals. Once placed on the ground a coverboard does its work with no maintenance. A coverboard's job is to serve as a microhabitat where mammals, reptiles, amphibians, and invertebrates can seek refuge but are not trapped or constrained in any way. If a critter is under the coverboard when you lift it, you are treated to a wildlife adventure. Often an unexpected one, like Sam's crowned snake discovery.

Anyone wanting to show kids animals that qualify as hidden biodiversity should put out a coverboard in their backyard or any site where they have permission to do so. We used three kinds of coverboards, with dimensions varying depending on what was available. Lots of herpetologists whose target is snakes choose sheets of roofing tin for coverboards. When snakes emerge from their winter refuges, many from underground, they want to bask in the sun to warm up on a cool day. Lying out in the open can be deadly if a passing hawk or other predatory bird sees the snake. Hiding under a piece of warming tin provides concealment. Tin in an open area can be a safe haven for snakes during cool days in autumn. During summer we find lizards such as racerunners and little brown skinks if the tin has not gotten too hot.

If your interest is in salamanders, especially in wet areas alongside a stream or in a swamp, pieces of thick plywood work best. Anyone setting out a two-by-two-foot coverboard around a vegetated section anywhere, even a backyard, will be almost certain to find some kind of animal to show a child. It might be just a beetle or an earwig or an earthworm. But most children are excited to see creatures they have not seen before. And something like a bessie bug beetle will probably stay under the same board for days.

Sheets of tar paper, known as poor-man's coverboards, can replace tin or wood. Tar paper is comparatively inexpensive coverboard material and is much lighter to transport. However, it deteriorates more quickly than either tin or plywood and must be replaced every few months. We have put out more than two hundred coverboards of tin, wood, and tarpaper in approximately equal numbers in woods, fields, and swamp. I have been able to show visitors in a single day as many as thirty different kinds of reptiles, amphibians, and small mammals hiding beneath coverboards at Salleyland. Parker once came back from the swamp carrying a five-pound snapping turtle he found buried in mud under a wooden coverboard.

Checking any coverboard is easy with the use of a snake stick, also called a stump ripper. Imagine a golf club with a four-to-five-inch metal prong at the business end that is perpendicular to the shaft. Ideally, one or more people stand on one side while the snake stick pulls up the tin, wood, or tarpaper to expose the substrate, and anything hiding beneath it. Natural cover of logs, ground litter, and rocks can be turned over as well. Environmental etiquette for turning over natural ground cover requires that you always place it back the way you found it. Anyone who wants to find many kinds of small animals without disrupting their habitat needs to give coverboards a try.

Swamp Jumpers Serve Two Purposes

Most swamps are difficult to walk through, hence the use of elevated boardwalks in many parks and other outdoor wildlife observation areas. I had no budget to construct a classic boardwalk, especially not if I complied with safety codes for handrails. However, slogging through a swamp with thick vegetation, hidden holes, and water levels that range from a muddy surface to a few inches of swamp water is difficult. To get from the wooded side of Salleyland to the field and sandhills requires a 150-yard trip across the stream and through the swamp. Nick the Builder had constructed a small bridge from the cabin side of the creek to the edge of the swamp. Now I had to figure out how we could cross the swamp from forest to sandhill habitat.

We designed a hybrid boardwalk/coverboard construction we call a "swamp jumper." Swamp jumpers serve a dual purpose: they provide a stable walking surface through mucky terrain and they act as coverboards before you step on them. I had two primary helpers in constructing the swamp jumpers, family friend Julian Lockwood and granddaughter Allison. Parker, Nick, and Sam carried a board or two, but Allison outdid them many times over in building the world's first swamp jumper boardwalk.

Julian is a masterful carpenter, but his skills were not needed for the simple walking surface we developed to traverse the often wet, always bumpy terrain. First we laid two 8-foot-long, 8-inch-wide, 2-inch-thick pressure-treated boards parallel to and flush against each other. Next we cut 3-foot-long two-by-fours and placed one under each pair of boards, about a foot from the end, which served as a perpendicular crosstie. The basic swamp jumper was born. Finally, we strategically positioned each swamp jumper so that the crossties sat on solid ground between pools of water or exposed roots, adding crossties as needed for proper balance. With Allison's help carrying boards and screwing them together with a battery-powered drill, the exercise culminated in a row of forty end-to-end swamp jumpers. Each was separated from the next by a short distance that allows a person to step from one to the next. We had built an easy walking path across the swamp.

Being in charge of logistics for this operation, I was the one Julian and Allison looked at with unspoken but presumed displeasure on the last day. We had just carried the final six hundred pounds of pressure-treated, southern yellow pine boards across the swamp from the cabin where I had delivered it. We had made several trips, walking on the already-in-place swamp jumpers. After seating the last pair of boards on dry land at the edge of the field, Allison said, "Grandpa, you could have driven your truck through the field right to this spot. We didn't need to carry all the boards across the swamp from the cabin."

I lamely replied that I felt it important to walk on the already placed swamp jumpers with a little weight to make sure each was stationary. More words went unspoken, but we all rejoiced that the swamp jumper boardwalk was now complete.

The swamp jumpers are not attached to each other, so each can be turned over as a single coverboard. We received many a questioning look from new visitors when they were told, "Don't step on the board. Turn it over first." Looks of consternation were sometimes visible when the only option was to step in the mud alongside the board. The system works great. Working together, the first two people use snake hooks at each end to turn over a swamp jumper and see if a prize awaits beneath. They then lower the swamp jumper back into place, taking care not to set the cross boards down on a scurrying salamander or jumping frog. By the end of the first year, during which we found more than two hundred salamanders of seven different species beneath well-seated swamp jumpers, no one remembered carrying some of the boards twice as far as we needed to. At least no one brought it up.

Our first swamp jumper walkway was joined by another after the leader of a Boy Scouts troop visited Salleyland. He needed an Eagle Scout project and had an idea. He proposed a path alongside the creek that would be built out of swamp jumpers. I liked the idea but doubted that it would ever get completed. The cost of the lumber and labor would be substantial. More onerous to me would be the paperwork involved in getting approval from various levels of the BSA bureaucracy. A year later, I signed a couple of forms and watched fourteen Boy Scouts unload a thousand feet of treated lumber and start laying out swamp jumpers. The grandkids and I were walking on them a few days later, seeing the creek close-up without tromping through the marginal vegetation. A few months after that we checked under the boards for the first time, without stepping on them beforehand—twelve salamanders, a broad-headed skink, and a DeKay's brown snake. Definitely a good start.

Make a Trashcan Trap

Tom Luhring invented the trashcan trap. Parker, Nick, Sam, Allison, and countless others have enjoyed using it. Tom used the aquatic collecting technique in his research on salamanders and published (with coauthor Chad Jennison) the description in the *Journal of Freshwater Ecology*. The trashcan trap has proved to be a valuable sampling tool for conducting research on salamanders and other aquatic animals. Its value in teaching people about the natural history of an aquatic area is virtually unsurpassed.

The basic design is relatively simple. Take a large, 32- to 44-gallon, heavy-duty plastic trashcan. Cut a 4-inch round hole on four sides with the bottom edge of each hole 2 inches from the bottom. A box cutter works well. Cut one 4-inch-wide, 8-inch-long rectangle with the short side starting a foot from the top. Drill a bunch of quarter-inch holes in the bottom of the trashcan; cut rectangles in the sides and cover them with window screen. The holes and screen will let water run out when the trashcan trap is lifted out of the water. Use quarter-inch hardware cloth to make funnels that fit in the circular openings of the 4-inch holes at the bottom. Drill small holes into the trashcan at appropriate spots and run zip ties through them to hold the window screen and hardware cloth funnels in place. Lower the trap into the water at a depth that allows animals to enter through the funnel openings but so that the top is several inches above the surface of the water. Leave the top that comes with the trashcan off while the trap is set so that animals are not permanently trapped inside. Any critter can get out eventually (or be eaten by something else) if you are not able to check the trap on a regular basis. The animal diversity that can be found in trashcan traps is remarkable.

One animal we have collected almost exclusively in trashcan traps is the bluespotted sunfish. The little fish is named after the males, which have dazzling blue spots on the body during breeding season. The females are not as colorful; they have numerous gold and greenish flecks in lieu of blue. If temperate zone fish were to replace brightly colored tropical ones in home aquariums, the bluespotted sunfish would be a top competitor.

Most animals that end up in trashcan traps are suitable for children and adults to handle. Tiny freshwater grass shrimp astonish anyone who thought all shrimp live in salt water. Pulling up a trap to find half a dozen bright red crawfish with claws apart and open, ready for battle, is always a delight. I enjoy teaching children (and adults) how to hold a crawfish behind the head. Seeing several brook silversides flopping around on the bottom of the trashcan is another thrill. The sleek little fish with a shiny stripe on each side are environmental indicators of a clear, flowing stream. Most of the lesser sirens at Salleyland have been captured in trashcan traps, one of the salamander species Tom Luhring designed the traps to catch.

Check Out Little Holes in the Ground

Searching for holes in the ground, from the quarter-inch diameter burrows of tiger beetle larvae to the foot-wide diggings of armadillos can be an educational exercise in itself. Every hole in the ground has a history, and finding out its origin and current occupants, if any, can lead to exciting wildlife discoveries. With a little bit of on-the-ground experience, someone can become fairly proficient at recognizing who dug what, and why.

Nick can definitely tell you who the little one-inch-diameter holes in a sandy oldfield belong to. We were standing in our abandoned agricultural field where we had planted sixteen thousand longleaf pine tree seedlings two years earlier when I handed him a shovel and said, "Dig right there where the hole is."

He did so, chipping away at the small tunnel disappearing into the sand. A minute later and a few feet away, three little mice popped out of the ground and scampered away through the underbrush. Nick looked disconcerted for a moment. "What were they? Where did they come from?"

The mouse-size holes with a little apron of sand outside belonged to a native mammal, the oldfield mouse. As Nick dug, the mice burst out of sandy soil a few feet away from where the hole was. Mike Smith, former director of SREL, had discovered as a graduate student many years ago that oldfield mice leave their home via an escape tunnel they dig upward from the underground burrow cavity. The escape route has no opening to the outside but ends an inch or so beneath the surface, allowing them to quickly push their way out if a snake or other predator enters the burrow looking for a meal.

You would never see an oldfield mouse in a person's house, although they look a bit like Jerry, the house mouse that constantly outsmarted Tom the cat in the classic cartoons. The oldfield mouse lives in sandy fields. One variety lives on beaches. Mammalogists cleverly call it the beach mouse. Oldfield mice come out only at night, venturing away from the open burrow entrance to forage for seeds in the field. During the day they huddle underground and nurse their babies until they are ready to come out on their own and begin foraging. Eventually the young leave their burrow home and start their own lives in their own burrows. Nick and I checked, and fortunately no babies were left behind in the burrow cavity, so all the little sand diggers were old enough to create new burrows nearby. Nick and I only dug up one burrow. My intent was not to destroy an animal's home but to show Nick how one of our native mammals lives at Salleyland.

Check Out Winter Plants

Shrubs with bright flowers and trees with chartreuse leaves abound in spring. In autumn other flowers and colorful leaves make an appearance. A winter field trip to observe nature in near-freezing weather can be uninspiring. To make a trip more meaningful I have on occasion asked a question: what do plants offer us in winter?

I took a February walk through the woods of Salleyland to appreciate the variety of plants to be seen and to look for native plants that remain green through the winter. With me were two excellent botanists, Linda Lee and retired biology professor Harry Shealy. Both are familiar with the names and biological secrets of native plants in the region.

In a suburban neighborhood, many yards have evergreens, including horticultural azaleas, camellias, and gardenias. The first camellias to arrive in the United States were brought here in the 1700s from England, descendants of ones originally imported from Asia. Common gardenias have a similar history. Both plants are products of centuries of work by enterprising horticulturists. No native plant belongs to either genus, and although biologically distinct, gardenias and camellias have something in common. They belong to plant families responsible for two of the most widely drunk beverages in the world. Gardenias are in the coffee family (Rubiaceae) and camellias are in the tea family (Theaceae).

Azaleas, once considered a separate group, are now included in the genus *Rhododendron*, in the heath family, the Ericaceae. Most evergreen azaleas seen in yards, along golf courses, and in city parks are horticultural varieties of Asian origin. Not all native azaleas stay green in winter. During our walk in the woods of Salleyland, we looked for and found several wild natives—swamp azaleas a.k.a. piedmont azaleas. These large shrubs are deciduous, losing their leaves in the fall but sporting beautiful pink and white flowers in early spring before they leaf out.

Whether native or introduced from another continent, whether evergreen or deciduous each member of these three plant families has a beauty of its own. I find evergreen plants in winter woods more interesting than those in a neighborhood. Natural forests comprise a higher diversity of trees, shrubs, and other plants with a variety of strategies to survive the transition from summer warmth to winter cold. In addition, the native plants are a vital support system for native animals of all sorts. Most plants in the woods are deciduous, dropping all their leaves in autumn. Brown and leafless plants can have their own appeal, but I wanted Linda and Harry to show me native plants that stay green all winter.

In my own woods, we narrowed the field of still-green trees pretty quickly—longleaf, shortleaf, and loblolly pines plus a few red cedar trees in a mostly hardwood forest. As we looked from the wooded hillside toward the swamp, tall loblolly pines stood out against the leafless maple, sweetgum, and tupelo gum trees. Most conifers, including firs, spruce, cedars, and pines, retain their green needles. Bald cypresses, which are also conifers, do not. I looked at a small, lonely bald cypress standing bare and needleless alongside the stream and wondered why it was different from its evergreen cousins. Botanists debate why some trees have evolved to lose their leaves and others to stay green. Why a short, seemingly lifeless bald cypress is never anyone's conifer of choice for a Christmas tree seems obvious.

Most temperate zone hardwoods like maples, flowering dogwoods, and hickories lose their leaves. But American holly, Carolina cherry laurel, and sweet bay magnolia stay green all year. We found them all that day, scattered through the woods down to the floodplain of the stream. Evergreen trees do shed their needles or leaves over time, replacing them with new ones. Brown pine needles and holly and magnolia leaves at the base of trees are evidence of continual replacement.

One of the most delightful evergreen plants growing throughout the shaded woods is called spotted wintergreen. I prefer the name Native Americans purportedly gave the small green-leaved plant with white vein-striping: pipsissewa. Little white flowers growing on stalks appear in late summer; the green leaves persist on the otherwise brown forest floor year-round. Having learned to locate pipsissewa, I look for them on every trip no matter what the season.

Another sure find in winter is Carolina jasmine, a green-leaved vine designated the South Carolina state flower in 1924. Jasmine vines are especially easy to locate in late winter because their bright yellow flowers are among the first to bloom in the area. The leaves and flowers are poisonous to eat, making beekeepers in the region wary of what jasmine honey might contain.

Field guides to the plants in your area offer information about native and introduced species. Having one with you can turn a walk around your neighborhood or through the woods into a learning adventure. Or you can just take a wintertime walk and admire nature's myriad wonders. You do not need to be a botanist to notice different ways plants deal with cold weather. But if you happen to know a couple of plant ecologists, invite them along for the walk.

Sam catches aquatic insects and a baby musk turtle with a dip net.
Photo by Jennifer G. High.

Embrace Serendipity

John Byrd and I stopped at the Beach for the birds. Several warblers and woodpeckers were in evidence, and then came a new sighting for Salleyland—a bald eagle flying upstream at treetop level. Very big bird when so close. We walked to the Powerline, and John noticed a small eastern kingsnake under the grass. First capture of a kingsnake at the land! I would not have seen it if John hadn't pointed it out. A day of serendipity at its best for eagles and kingsnakes.

SALLEYLAND FIELD NOTES, NOVEMBER 16, 2015

SCIENTISTS, SCHOOLTEACHERS, AND SCIENCE FAIRS PUT A LOT OF EMPHA-sis on testing hypotheses as part of the so-called scientific method. The scientific method includes a fundamental and necessary first step that precedes any hypothesis: observation. Before a hypothesis can even be proposed a question must be formulated based on prior observation. Toward this end, much, if not most, knowledge and advancement of natural history phenomena start as an outcome of serendipity. Serendipity, a pleasing, unplanned encounter, can turn any stroll in the woods, trip down a stream, slog through a swamp, or walk across a field into a memorable outdoor experience. Most snakes and other wildlife are serendipitous discoveries, often enhanced by experience but never assured. Observations, questions, and testable hypotheses may ensue. But merely learning something new about plants or animals might be a likely by-product from an unexpected revelation and be as enlightening as a well-done experiment designed to test a hypothesis.

As a retired ecologist, I find relying on the fruits of serendipity quite gratifying. Designing and conducting experiments to support or disprove a hypothesis may result in definitive answers to some questions, but trusting to serendipity is much more fun. The following are some of our by-chance observations. The next steps of proposing hypotheses and testing them I will leave to others who are in academic situations where they are judged on the process.

Phantom Crane Flies Live Up to Their Name

What's your favorite insect? Butterflies, dragonflies, and damselflies would certainly be in most people's top 10. Praying mantises and walking sticks are also popular choices. Among beetles, the largest group of insects in the world, some top contenders are June bugs, ladybugs, and click beetles. Katydids and tree crickets might make the cut for folks who enjoy musical night sounds. And for nighttime sights, lightning bugs top the list. Honeybees would be the choice of some with a more practical bent. If the phantom crane fly were better known it would surely be a contender.

Sam, Nick, and I watched these peculiar creatures in the swamp one June as they drifted over an area of dark mud. They have tiny wings, but their primary means of aerial flotation comes from their six long legs, some segments of which are expanded and filled with breathing tubes. The legs extend outward from the body like wheel spokes to catch the faintest breeze. Phantom crane flies appear to float through the air. Their legs are alternating bands of black and white so that as they move from sunlight to shadow the dark markings disappear and only the lighter color is visible. If you are alongside a swamp and see an eerie specter of white dots drifting silently through the air, like part of a wafting spiderweb, you are probably looking at a floating phantom crane fly, a mesmerizing sight.

Crane flies belong to the order Diptera, the true flies, which are estimated by some entomologists to have more than a million species. But in contrast to some of their kin, such as mosquitoes, horseflies, and houseflies with hundreds or thousands of species, those in the phantom crane fly family number only a handful. In the eastern United States most belong to a single species. Another distinction between these elegant spirits of the swamp and many other Diptera is that they are completely inoffensive. No biting, no buzzing, no stinging. If you are fortunate enough to have one land on your arm, it may depart like a dandelion blowball with the next puff of wind before you can even photograph it.

Put phantom crane flies on your list of harmless wildlife to look for on your next stroll near a swamp, stream, or other natural wetland area with trees overhead that make it dark during the day. In my experience, they stay low to the ground, and a mucky surface, where they lay their eggs for larvae to hatch before developing into pupae, is the preferred habitat. The larvae thrive on bits of decaying vegetation and diatoms, a type of algae. These are among the ingredients that make up what we call swamp mud. We should never be judgmental about a natural habitat, even if we find it yucky, because virtually all are important to some living organisms. We should also appreciate all scavengers of the natural world, including vultures, opossums, and phantom crane flies. Without them, the world would be an unpleasant place to live. On the flip side, I doubt if any predator makes a living eating adult phantom crane flies although the larvae are probably tasty to other denizens of swamp mud.

Once you develop a search image for phantom crane flies, you will be able to locate them readily if they are present. They drift at the mercy of the wind, with tiny wings and contrasting black and white banding on the legs, and none will move faster than you walk unless the wind is more than a breeze. Our natural habitats have much to offer for those who take the time to look. If you don't see a phantom crane fly on your visit to the edge of a dark wetland, check out the other sights and sounds around you. You might find a new favorite insect.

Another Solar Eclipse Is Coming Soon

We were lucky. The strip of totality was scheduled to cross right over our property, with a full eclipse lasting for almost two minutes. Any astronomer would argue that being in the right place at the right time was not really a serendipitous event as the prediction could have been made centuries earlier. But a year earlier I had no idea a total eclipse and I would be in the same place at the same time.

You won't have to wait long for the next solar eclipse, which will happen every day of every year. You just will not be in the right place to see it, because most of the zones of totality will be in outer space and not on Earth. Except for the few hours of lunar eclipses (when Earth is between the moon and the sun) a solar eclipse is happening constantly. The moon is casting a shadow somewhere out there all the time, except when it's hiding behind our planet.

Seeing a full solar eclipse is spectacular, and in August 2017 the nation responded to the opportunity from coast to coast and even in the ocean when a shadowy swath crossed the continent from Oregon to South Carolina, moving across the landscape at a speed of more than a thousand miles an hour. A cruise ship destined for the zone of totality offshore was booked weeks in advance. Thousands drove to locations hundreds of miles away where they were assured of a view of the sun being totally blacked out for two minutes or more. Well, assuming the weather cooperated by providing a clear sky.

I wanted to know what animals would do, so I invited a dozen friends to join us in our field for a pre-eclipse picnic and a guaranteed 1 minute and 57 seconds of no sun. We made no assurances about the weather, other than promising high temperatures and humidity, except for the ten-degree drop in temperature during totality. The capricious nature of clouds was understandably out of our control.

To observe behavior of different species, I asked people to tune in to selected animal groups. An ornithologist was to watch and listen to what nearby birds did. Another individual was to pay attention to calling insects, especially nocturnal tree crickets and katydids. Lots of dragonflies were flying around in the field, so some guests were asked to see if they stopped flying and perched on vegetation. I elected to watch our two beehives to see what the bees did. As for the flora, I didn't need to be an ecologist to know a two-minute eclipse would be inconsequential to plants, so no one was put in charge of the grass, shrubs, or trees.

To have a record of the eclipse itself, we invited a first-rate photographer, Mark Vukovich, with a camera as long as my arm to capture the full solar eclipse, including corona and solar flares. And everyone took pictures of others in the group as they leaned back in lawn chairs and stared sunward with funky-looking glasses. Fortunately, we had blue sky for half an hour before and after the eclipse.

Observations in our field were interesting but not breathtaking. Four mourning doves flew up into a tree, which is not particularly instructive as they fly into trees on a regular basis every day. The person in charge of dragonflies became distracted by the celestial events underway and forgot to see what they or any other insects did. One unequivocal change in animal behavior just before total eclipse was that honeybees returned to the hives in droves, presumably responding to being caught off guard with an unexpected sunset. They were out again minutes later as light returned. I doubt any of them wasted any pollen-gathering time trying to figure out why the night had been such a short one.

I later talked with Scott Pfaff, curator of herpetology at Riverbanks Zoo and Garden in Columbia, South Carolina, to find out how zoo animals responded to the total eclipse. At the zoo, observations were equally

J. D. Willson looks on as Allison, Parker, and the author hold a black racer retrieved from under a tin coverboard. Photo by Mike Gibbons.

underwhelming. The giant tortoises placidly eating grass on the lawn outside the reptile house continued to do so during total darkness and afterward. Alligators and aquatic turtles did not move from where they basked or floated. The main behavioral observation was that the flock of flamingos at the zoo began running wildly—not because of a two-minute period of darkness but because they were terrified when the ten thousand visitors at the zoo gave a loud cheer when the sun disappeared. Not an unreasonable response for any being.

My conclusion as an ecologist about animal responses is that the species most responsive to and dramatically affected by a total eclipse is one of the primates—humans, the only animal to be aware of an eclipse before it happens.

Visit the Swamp at Night

"Awesome," was the only word Nick uttered when he saw the spectacle. It was an awesome experience for me as well. Not only to see what we were seeing but to be where we were when we saw it.

The request from a fearless seven-year-old "to go out in the swamp at night" was one any self-respecting granddad would have honored. So Nick and I planned a weekend at our cabin in the woods.

Sunset will be at 8:27 p.m., or so he informed me, apparently having acquired the background information we needed. By 7:00 p.m. he had gathered flashlights and suited up in a pair of children's chest waders. Nothing like getting ready ahead of time. I took charge at that point and declared that I must have a cup of coffee, since it was still daylight. When we started our trek an hour later, I had put on rubber hip boots. A lingering twilight filled the sky that gradually darkened as we walked through two-foot-high cinnamon ferns over terrain that varied from lush carpets of emerald green sphagnum moss to clear pools of foot-deep water. Flashlights were not really necessary at first. When total darkness descended, we turned our flashlights on.

I led the way, with Nick following a few feet behind. When we came to water, he held onto my back pocket lest he trip or we hit a deeper pool. We stopped occasionally to turn off the flashlights and listen to the sounds of the swamp. "Cool," said Nick when we heard the commanding sounds of two barred owls challenging each other for dominion over that part of the swamp. We heard a cricket frog, whose call Nick likened to someone hitting two marbles together. Then we heard a loud chorus of green treefrogs, their quacking sounding more like ducks than frogs. I suggested we go find them.

We walked and waded along, shining our flashlights carefully ahead of our path as I parted vegetation. I was hoping to find a cottonmouth but with plenty of time to see it and watch it, not step on it. Once we saw a banded watersnake slither into a dark pool and disappear. We finally reached an area of standing water where we were surrounded by noisy green treefrogs. We couldn't see them, but they were all around us. Many frogs are ventriloquists, making it difficult to be sure of the exact direction of a single one. When a chorus of a dozen or more are calling, tracking individuals becomes an auditory head-turning event, and the surround-sound adds to one's confusion about where the calls are coming from. Then Nick saw one calling from the stem of a broadleaf arrowhead plant standing in shallow water. He moved stealthily and with the skill of a professional grabbed it. We looked it over, agreed that it was a beautiful animal with its brilliant green back and white racing stripe down each side, and released it back on one the big plant leaves of the plant. It was now late, time to head back.

As we walked on solid ground along a ridge with swamp on both sides,

Nick learns how to hold a banded watersnake without getting bitten.
All the grandchildren can identify the snakes at Salleyland and know
never to pick up a venomous one. Photo by Mike Gibbons.

I proposed that we stop one more time and turn off our flashlights. This
time we heard the upbeat call of a chuck-will's-widow, a close kin of the
whip-poor-will. We paused for a minute more, staring at total blackness
all around, and then it happened. One of the most amazing insect displays
imaginable. Lightning bugs. Hundreds upon hundreds of lightning bugs
flashing their signals. But these were not the everyday (or night) random
glimmers of backyard lightning bugs. These fireflies were flashing in unison,
in total synchrony. One moment the swamp was on fire with twinkling bio-
luminescence. The next instant the inky black night enveloped us. Then the
fireflies lit up the swamp again.

In *Fireflies, Glow-worms, and Lightning Bugs*, Lynn Faust describes several species of lightning bugs whose males collectively produce their flashing
courtship displays synchronously. Mating is the game, and each species has
its own unique pattern of blinking to which only females of that species re-
spond. Hundreds of people sign up for programmed visits each year during
the few nights when the synchronous fireflies are displaying at Allegheny

National Forest in Pennsylvania; Congaree National Park in South Carolina; and the one considered by many to be the "most famous," Elkmont, Tennessee, in Great Smoky Mountains National Park.

I'm quite certain the display Nick and I saw at Salleyland was every bit as spectacular as any of the others. I have seen the synchronous firefly phenomenon three times in other swamps. The biological explanation for why the males blink synchronously remains a mystery. But you do not need to know why to know that the dazzling sight is indeed "awesome."

Everybody Recognizes a Hornet's Nest

A few things in nature are so distinctive that no one is likely to confuse them with another life-form. A box turtle, a big red mushroom, and a hornet's nest are three such things. Fortunately for me, Parker pointed out the hornet's nest before I walked into it face-first. The two-foot-long, football-shaped paper structure looked like a piñata hanging head-high in the woods. The first step to enjoying a bald-faced hornet's nest is to be aware of it before you bump your head on it.

These members of the yellow jacket family will protect their nest by repeatedly attacking and stinging anything perceived as a threat. Our German shepherd once ventured too close to a nest and half a dozen winged black-and-white defenders swarmed out of the nest opening like bullets, all finding their mark. On this occasion, Parker and I watched from about fifteen feet away as hornets landed at the entrance and entered the nest while others were coming out. I thought about pitching a little stick to jiggle the nest and see what would happen, but I was overcome by a wave of sanity when I realized I wasn't positive I could outrun my grandson.

Bald-faced hornets are the largest North American yellow jackets. An entomologist would be quick to tell you that they are not true hornets like the European and Asian species, but let's call them hornets anyway. They are certainly large enough to qualify, being almost an inch long, but they do not sport the characteristic black-and-yellow banding of the smaller varieties. In flight they look mostly black with light markings. Head-on the face looks like a fierce mask of ebony and ivory. And they don't just look ferocious. Bald-faced hornets feed not only on nectar, pollen, and tree sap but also on insects, including large ones such as cicadas and praying mantises. The most ambitious predatory takedown for one of these hornets, documented in British Columbia, was a rufous hummingbird! The geographic range of bald-faced hornets includes all of the contiguous United States and southern Canada.

The life cycle of this fascinating animal is complex in some ways but relatively straightforward in others. In early spring, when sustained warm weather appears certain, female bald-faced hornets emerge from winter dormancy and each selects a nest site. Some nests are low to the ground like the one we found hanging at eye-level; others may be more than fifty feet high in a tree. The female builds a small wasp-like, honey-combed nest and lays an egg in each cell. The hatching hornets are all infertile females that immediately begin expanding the nest by chewing wood and mixing it with their saliva, which acts like starch on a cotton shirt. Using their legs, they begin shaping what will become the hive.

The queen meanwhile lays more eggs, producing a larger workforce. The process continues until the nest is finished; it will serve as home for the colony of around four hundred wasps. As autumn approaches, the queen alters the egg-laying process to produce fertile offspring—males, called drones, and females that will be the future queens. Mating occurs before cold weather sets in, producing new queens that seek hiding places beneath ground and in rotten logs and tree cavities. At year's end the queens are the only survivors; all the workers and drones have died.

A hornet's nest is an amazing piece of natural architecture that can be collected and preserved without harming nature. By the first frosts, almost all the workers have perished, the queens have departed, and the unattended nests will soon be damaged by winter winds and rains. Unlike honeybees that use the same hive the following year, a bald-faced hornet's nest is abandoned, despite the effort that went in to building it. It is quite acceptable to remove it from its environment. Be sure to pick a cold day, because any remaining female workers will defend the nest till the very end. Drones are not a problem; they have no stingers. Come cold weather, the hornet's nest we had found made a great show-and-tell at Parker's school.

Learn to Enjoy Spiders

Parker is captivated by spiders. Like snakes and sharks, spiders induce in people a range of emotions from deep-seated fear to intense interest. I used to dread them, to a point approaching arachnophobia, the deep, irrational fear of spiders. Now I think they are marvelous beings. I did not get over my fear of spiders until I was in college, several decades ago, during a memorable encounter with one in the wild. A colleague urged me to pick up a Texas brown tarantula with a leg span larger than my hand. After letting it walk up my arm and over my shoulder, I finally let my breath out as my companion removed the spider and let it go. The spider spell was broken. Parker accomplished this first step in elementary school. His appreciation of these eight-legged animals now leans toward arachnophilia.

Most spiders are exquisite creatures; they get a bad rap from a few troublemakers. Even so, threats to humans from the black widow and brown recluse are vastly overrated. Although either could potentially deliver a serious bite, documentation of deaths from either are vanishingly rare, if not nonexistent, except under unusual circumstances. Of the more than thirty-five thousand species of spiders, most have fangs and can inject venom. But most are too small to deliver a memorable bite to humans.

At Salleyland we welcome spiders as heralds of environmental health, as should everyone everywhere. Spiders are top carnivores. When spiders are thriving, plants and animals lower on the food chain must also be doing well. Spiders, with their interweaving connections to their environment, are a sign that at least some portion of the ecosystem is operating properly.

I really like spiders, and I consider it a good sign when I receive a question about arachnids that refers to a "beautiful spider." Or when a neighbor wanted me to see her "pet spider on the breakfast room window." The black-and-yellow garden spider's web, fully two feet across and covering the window, could not have been better placed for an all-day gladiator show from inside the house. These wonderful creatures build the quintessential spiderweb of concentric circles with spokes from the center. They and their webs are indeed quite beautiful. We consider any spider we find at Salleyland as a desirable neighbor.

People who accept, or better yet appreciate, spiders have what I consider a healthy enthusiasm for the natural world. I'm not sure why anyone would want to get rid of a spider that is not inside the house, and maybe not even then. If you watch them carefully you will soon see that a fascinating group of animals lives right in your neighborhood. I'm not suggesting you go around picking up spiders, regardless of whether you are afraid of them, though I have watched Parker and my sister JoLee pick up a gigantic wolf spider and let it scamper across their hands. "It's the biggest spider I've ever seen," said Nick. But he is not afraid of them either. In the field of arachnology, Parker, Nick, and Sam are clearly way ahead of where I was at their age, and I am unlikely to catch up.

Spiders are predators and watching them bring down prey can be exciting. Nick and I watched a variable dancer damselfly flit into the web of a beautiful marbled orb weaver. The web was strategically placed in a sun/shade area at the edge of the swamp. The marbled orb weaver, with its intricate yellow, white, and black abdomen and orange legs, was soon devouring its midday meal. Not the same as watching a lion bring down a gazelle? True, but the predator-prey principle is the same. And the spider-damselfly interaction has been seen by few people. The food web drama continued later when we saw a green anole attack and subdue a small wolf spider.

Spider sagas are fascinating and include more than basic predator-prey interactions. Upon turning over a piece of tin in the field, I found a magnificent insect known as the rusty spider wasp with a red body and blue wings. Beside it lay an upside-down wolf spider on the dirt where the wasp had dug a small depression. The females of these solitary wasps attack large spiders as they travel overland. But they sting to paralyze, not kill. They drag the listless spider to a safe harbor where they dig out a depression, place the spider in it, and then lay an egg. When the wasp egg hatches, the larva feeds on the still living spider. Where do you suppose someone came up with the outrageous idea for *Alien*?

Over the years Parker has discovered dozens of kinds of spiders, each with its own suite of remarkable behaviors and lifestyles. To fool predators that would eat a spider but avoid ants, ant-mimic spiders look like ants. Some even hold up their front legs to look like antennae. One August, Parker found a funnel web spider that had attached its web to the inside of the screen door to the porch. For weeks, we used the other door so as not to disturb it.

Later that same month, Allison found an enormous dark fishing spider on the cabin porch. Sam, Nick, Parker, and I watched as it stealthily approached an active nest of red paper wasps. The nest was a small one under the eaves with about half a dozen inhabitants. When the spider was about a foot away, one of the wasps attacked it, and then another. The fishing spider warded off these two attacks and a few more with its many legs flailing in the air. It eventually rappelled on a strand down to the railing where we watched it go over and disappear, presumably in search of less aggressive prey. Parker found several different spiders over the summer, including a variety of wolf spiders, basilica orb weavers, golden silk orb weavers, yellow garden spiders, trapdoor spiders, and long-jawed orb weavers. On one moonless night he discovered that some spiders can be located by their eye-shine in a flashlight beam.

I consider spiders to be one of the most underappreciated creatures on Earth. They have much to offer anyone with an appetite to enjoy the wildlife smorgasbord to the fullest. Go find as many spiders as you can and discover their secrets.

Some Crane Flies Look like Giant Mosquitoes

Sam pointed at the huge insect, saying, "That's the biggest mosquito I've ever seen." I knew it was a crane fly, not a mosquito, but I too had something to learn about these fascinating insects.

Like mosquitoes, crane flies have six long legs, two wings, a little head, and a long abdomen. But some crane flies are ten times as large as any mosquito. And they do not bite people. Nor do they sting. Crane flies are only looking for one of the opposite sex to mate with. Most do not eat anything as adults.

We were walking through the swamp, turning over coverboards and checking the vegetation for resting insects and possibly a lizard. Sam looked into the center of a stump and pointed out the large insect. At first we thought it was caught in a spiderweb. It bounced rapidly back and forth from one plant leaf to another several inches away like a bug trying to escape the strand of a spiderweb but without touching either leaf. On further inspection we saw that it was airborne on its own, with wings whirring so fast they were only a blur. Whether the erratic flight pattern is a mating ritual or a mechanism to avoid becoming lunch for a passing bird, the behavior is definitely eye-catching.

When the creature finally stopped, we looked to see if it had any distinguishing features. Hundreds of different kinds of crane flies live in North America, so I was not expecting to determine the species. But this one was so big, I thought we might see some anatomical peculiarity or coloration of interest. And Sam did—it had a red head. Being otherwise nondescript dull brown or gray, like mosquitoes, why would a crane fly have a bright red head? Among many insect species, males and females have different color patterns, but I had never seen a crane fly with red coloration. I took a close-up cell phone photo.

The legs of crane flies and the tails of lizards have a trait in common. Both have joints with what are called fracture zones that make them break off easily. When a predator grabs a crane fly or a lizard, it may end up with only part of a leg or part of a tail while the rest of the animal escapes. Because they are such fragile insects, we decided just to observe it. I had a photo we could examine later.

When we enlarged the photo, we saw that the red coloration was not a body part on the crane fly itself but a cluster of globules that looked like little eggs. Animals do some strange things, so nothing is off the table, especially when it comes to reproductive behavior. Nonetheless, a review of a few scientific journals came up with other possibilities for why we had seen a redheaded crane fly. Our best guess was that the insect had tiny phoretic mites that had collected on its head. "Phoresis" is an ecological term for one animal transporting another. The crane fly was carrying the mites.

Mites are arachnids, like spiders and scorpions, and many make a living as parasites on other animals. Like varroa mites that are parasites on honeybees, phoretic mites can cause serious problems for some insects. But some phoretic mites use insects simply as free transportation from one area to another where their true target for feeding is. One study in Japan revealed that crane flies transported phoretic mites to mushrooms that the mites fed on.

Nature is full of symbiotic relationships. Some are mutualistic (both organisms benefit), some commensalistic (one organism benefits, the other is unharmed), some parasitic (one benefits, the other is harmed), and some are a combination. Were the mites we saw traveling atop the crane using the insect as a taxi service? Or was the crane fly itself the food source for the little demons? The answer is unclear, which in no way detracted from the pleasure we had observing the crane fly.

Set Wildlife Cameras

I arrived with a stinking, blood-splattered deer. I had a South Carolina DNR-issued salvage permit for collecting biological specimens
in case someone challenged why I was picking up a road-killed doe
on a fairly busy highway. I set out the deer along SNAP Road and
secured its head and legs to nearby trees with rope to keep big scavengers from dragging it away. Three turkey vultures, which can smell
decaying flesh, circled overhead. I set up four wildlife cameras, pointing from different angles. I heard barred owls across the creek and
wondered if they would also be interested in a dead deer.

SALLEYLAND FIELD NOTES, JANUARY 29, 2018

DURING THE PAST FEW DECADES, ONE OF THE BIGGEST EYE-OPENERS IN
wildlife ecology has come from one of the simplest technologies—
wildlife cameras, also called trail cameras. Both video and still frame wildlife
cameras have been used by hunters and wildlife ecologists for many years.
The former want to determine when and where the best hunting opportunities are for game species. Wildlife researchers, on the other hand, assess
what animals inhabit an area in order to make management recommenda-
tions or simply to better understand the biodynamics of a habitat and estimate population abundances, feeding patterns, and general behavior of various species. In other words, to understand the basic ecology of the animals.
Improved technology and greater affordability have made wildlife cameras
accessible to the general populace. After my kids gave me one for a birthday present, I developed a new appreciation for what lives in our woods and
along our stream that we seldom encounter in person.

Our list of wildlife residents has grown significantly since we began capturing videos and still shots of nocturnal visitors to our cabin in the woods.

We had seen several deer as well as their trails and other signs. But catching them on camera almost every time we put out corn has revealed they are much more abundant than is readily apparent. The same phenomenon has proved to be true in many suburban areas where I encourage friends to put out wildlife cameras. Almost all are surprised to learn that their neighborhoods, especially those bordering natural wooded habitats, have numerous night travelers that we seldom or never see, including a couple of top-tier eastern predators—bobcats and coyotes.

One reason for deer being revealed on a wildlife camera is because most deer are active at night, and the wildlife cameras are equipped with infrared night vision or a white flash or both. Likewise, with armadillos. We find their diggings numerous places around the woods but only occasionally spot an active one out during the day. The wildlife cameras make it clear that armadillos are abundant and ubiquitous on the property. We seldom see them because they come out primarily at night.

Wildlife Cameras Reveal Hidden Biodiversity

I watched two fat beavers sitting side by side, eating from a pile of corn while three raccoons walked around them eating kernels off to either side. Clearly the beavers had the prime spot in the center of the corn but none of the animals seemed to be paying attention to the others. Beavers held the dominant role not because they are cute butterballs but because they have much bigger teeth. I was watching this supper scene unfold on my computer after downloading photos from a wildlife camera. I had put the corn out on the ground as bait two days before.

Raccoons intrigue me. They are simultaneously ubiquitous, abundant, and covert, with the ability to stay out of sight during the day. I have night photos of six together at one corn pile. They were joined by two deer and an opossum. The animals did not interact. They simply ignored each other. The next day we were unable to spot any of the night visitors. Where do they all go?

Among our favorite early surprises captured by the wildlife camera were a bobcat walking across a beaver dam, a southern flying squirrel landing on a tree trunk, and a red-shouldered hawk taking a bath in the creek. One of the best action shots was of a barred owl that landed on a stump the camera was pointed toward. In the owl's talons was a salamander known as a siren. The photograph was published by the Southeastern Outdoor Press with the

A beaver and two male wood ducks share a section of the creek near the cabin where loose corn has been scattered. Photo by author.

caption "Day and Night." The rationale for the title was a daytime scene at the same spot the following day: a great blue heron standing in the water and a pair of wood ducks swimming by at the same time. The heron may have been trying its hand at finding one of the sirens that the barred owl had proved were present. Your own yard might reveal unsuspected guests, both day and night.

When Parker got a wildlife camera for his birthday, he set it up facing a small, active beaver dam at Salleyland. The following week we found out who came to the dam: a slider turtle basking, two raccoons walking across, and an aimless opossum who seemed uncertain whether to cross or just look at the water. Parker had first tested the camera in our backyard. Among the expected inhabitants were a neighbor's house cat at night and a dog during the day. He was surprised to see a pair of raccoons and an opossum in the backyard at night. Wild animals are obviously all around us, whether in the woods or in suburbia.

Finding out that seldom-seen native animals are present in your area can be exciting. Some animals may be more spectacular than others. But I am not intimidated by what friends and colleagues discover during their field studies in southern Florida, Arizona, and Alaska. Sure, mountain lions, bears, and moose are impressive. But I am content to enjoy capturing a sighting of whatever we have lurking around that we rarely see. And think about it: how often are you likely to see beavers sharing a smorgasbord with raccoons? Probably never if mountain lions and bears are around to join them for supper.

Fox Squirrels Are Impressive

Jim Beasley, wildlife biologist at the University of Georgia and SREL, and Jim High both claimed to have seen a fox squirrel at Salleyland. Their sightings were independent, and I believed both of them but had not confirmed the presence of fox squirrels myself. Their claims were vindicated when I finally got several clear wildlife camera photographs of a fox squirrel on a tree alongside a duck box near the cabin. Like most fox squirrels in our region it looked like a gray squirrel with a black head but was much bigger.

Fox squirrels are one of our native North American tree squirrels and the closest relative to the well-known gray squirrel. Although the two species differ in size, appearance, and a few aspects of ecology and behavior, their biology is similar in many ways. Both occupy the same regions throughout most of the eastern United States, with gray squirrels ranging farther north, including into New England, and fox squirrels occurring as far west as Montana and Wyoming. Although both species can be found in parts of southern Canada, neither hibernates, relying on stores of acorns and other nuts that they cache during warmer months to get through a cold winter.

The two most obvious physical differences between fox squirrels and gray squirrels are body size and coloration. Numerous studies by wildlife biologists indicate that gray squirrels are much smaller, ranging in total length of tail and body from about 15 inches to less than 21 inches, the maximum size ever reported. Typical weights for gray squirrels range from less than 12 ounces to a maximum of 26 ounces. Fox squirrels commonly reach total lengths between 18 and 27 inches. They are also much heavier, weighing from 18 ounces to 4 pounds, more than twice as much as the largest gray squirrels.

Coat color is usually a sure way to distinguish a gray squirrel from a fox squirrel. The standard light gray color pattern of the former is familiar to anyone living in the eastern part of the country. However, some gray squirrels have a reddish or cinnamon color, and occasional populations may be solid black. Fox squirrels vary much more in color throughout their range. Particular color patterns are characteristic of certain localities and regions. In parts of the Carolinas and Georgia, a large squirrel that has a black body with white ears and feet or a silver body with a black head is a fox squirrel. In many parts of their geographic range, including Alabama, Mississippi, and Indiana, fox squirrels are more commonly tan, orange, or even reddish in coloration. Some wildlife biologists have tried to use geographical variation in body color for taxonomic classification, but one research study concluded that fur color varies too much geographically for the trait to be used to categorize them as different subspecies. In other words, a fox squirrel with black, silver, tan, or orange fur might show up in any part of its range.

One reason for the rarity of fox squirrel sightings is that they require a much larger area of habitat than do their smaller cousins, which have a significantly greater population density. Wildlife studies in several southern and midwestern states found numerous gray squirrel populations ranging from 350 to 3,500 individuals per square mile. Comparable censuses of fox squirrels seldom yielded more than 100 per square mile. According to one report, fox squirrels have been reduced in population size by half or more in many parts of their natural range due to habitat loss, especially old growth forests. The fox squirrel is a federally endangered species in parts of Delaware, Maryland, and Virginia. In my experience, beyond the occasional chance encounter with a fox squirrel in the woods, you are most likely to see them along the edges of golf courses and parkways. I was delighted to confirm the fox squirrel as one of our marvelous native wildlife inhabitants at Salleyland.

What Lives in the Hollow Holly?

When we walk north from our cabin in the woods, we pass a big tree we call the Hollow Holly. We always poke a stick inside to see if anything will run out. Nothing has. Yet.

Any nature-oriented person would be intrigued by the almost fifty-foot-tall American holly. Two feet in diameter, its gray-barked trunk is covered below by a skirt of bright emerald green moss. Ruby red holly berries against sharp-pointed dark green leaves are a pretty sight in winter. But the real attraction of this tree is a large, cave-like opening at the base with an apron of soft dirt marked by many animal tracks. On the inside, three well-used burrows, each large enough to accommodate a small opossum, lead away from the hollowed-out base in different directions. The tree is unquestionably the home, or at least a stopover site, for wildlife.

We decided to find out what visits the Hollow Holly by setting up wildlife cameras aimed at the trail and at the base of the tree trunk. Hunters, ecologists, and wildlife biologists have specific reasons for using wildlife cameras. We just wanted to see what happens at the Hollow Holly.

Turns out a lot happens when we are not there. We recorded seven different mammalian visitors. On the first night the camera was set up, an armadillo entered the opening and disappeared down one of the tunnels without hesitation. Presumably, we had witnessed one of the original architects of the burrow system. Later in the evening, an adult eastern woodrat emerged from a different tunnel. Woodrats are large native rodents with chubby bodies and somewhat furry tails. The Hollow Holly is probably home for a family of woodrats.

Around midnight, three raccoons moved over the ground in front of the hollow. One disappeared into it and came out a minute or so later. A passing opossum later did the same thing. Were they checking for an easy insect meal inside the tree or did they have a room in the wildlife apartment complex? A white-tailed deer, a young buck, stuck its head into the photo frame, sniffing the grass and chewing a blade. It turned its head and looked in the tree hollow as if curious what might be inside. The most impressive visitor showed up around 4:00 a.m., just after an opossum left, which was fortunate timing for it. A huge bobcat appeared, stuck its head inside the hole like someone peering into a refrigerator wondering what there was to eat, looked around, and left. At early light, a pair of gray squirrels came into view, not from under the tree but from above, and foraged around in front of the opening at the base. Even an old stump may be somebody's home.

Revealing wildlife's hidden biodiversity brings a greater appreciation for natural habitats in a region. Knowing that our little woodland habitat has such a rich assortment of mammals is not only gratifying but also exciting, although we seldom experience any of the nocturnal animals face-to-face. The educational lessons that can be learned from a wildlife camera are many.

Here is the most important lesson for everyone, especially commercial developers, land managers, and anyone interested in conservation of native wildlife: when we destroy habitat, we destroy the homes and haunts of wildlife that live there even though we may never see them. The Hollow Holly is living proof that our woodland communities are full of fascinating treasures that may be out of sight but that should never be put out of mind.

Why Would a Fox Enjoy a Dead Opossum?

When I saw the fox stick its face into a road-killed opossum and then roll around on its back to get a thorough coating of the dead animal smell, I was reminded of every dog I have ever had. To watch a dog squirm around on top of a rotting animal or other disgusting item is to observe one of their most undesirable behaviors, from a human perspective. Watching a fox perform the act was fascinating, as it would not be coming home with me to jump on the couch.

Observing the fox's enthusiastic behavior upon finding a dead opossum did not happen by chance. I had put the road-killed opossum at the edge of the field bordering our woods two days earlier and set up a wildlife camera to see who would visit. Using fresh roadkill to set up a scavenger feeding station is like putting sunflower seeds in a bird feeder. Tossing a steady supply of dead opossums, coons, and gray squirrels into your backyard in town is not recommended. Though you might enjoy the show, your neighbors are likely to be less enthusiastic. Setting up a scavenger buffet in a remote rural habitat is acceptable, and the customers, who come mostly at night, except for vultures and hawks, are generally more interesting than blue jays and house finches.

In viewing the photos, I was interested to see that wild foxes can exhibit the same behavior as dogs when they find a smelly mess on the ground. I wondered why they do so. Scent rolling, as it is called, did not evolve simply as a pointless exercise that members of the dog family engage in when they are bored and want to annoy their owner. Presumably, the behavior in domestic dogs is a purposeless holdover from their wild ancestors. But for foxes and other wild animals, the action must have a function, although behavioral biologists do not agree on what it might be.

Some wildlife biologists posit that wolves roll on carrion or animal droppings to bring information back to the pack about the presence in the vicinity of a prey species, such as deer or elk. A predator might also be providing evidence to a mate of its own prowess at finding prey. Likewise, being made aware of a competing species or predator nearby might be useful. A fox might take it as a warning if its mate came home smelling like bobcat or coyote dung.

Another proposal has been that a fox may mask or camouflage its own scent when sneaking up on a rabbit or mouse. Of course, one has to wonder about any prey animal that would not be alarmed upon smelling a long-dead opossum approaching, so I'm not enamored with that hypothesis. Another suggestion has been that a predator might roll around on a dead animal in order to mark its territory by leaving its own smell. But would a live animal's scent be detectable above the overpowering smell of a rotting carcass? Possibly to another fox. One idea is that to dogs, wolves, and foxes the sense of smell is dominant, and they may enjoy putting on a new scent the way some people like to stand out with their choice of perfume, jewelry, or unconventional clothing.

My appreciation for wildlife cameras has grown immeasurably with the realization that they not only show me what is in the area but also reveal normally unseen behaviors. When we uncover wildlife's hidden biodiversity and observe what it is doing, we enter a new realm of understanding and appreciation for the natural habitats that surround us.

Conduct a Mammal Survey

Taxonomic groups differ greatly in how the presence of a species is documented. Chance encounters are always possible but confirming whether a certain species is present in a habitat of interest or prescribed area of land usually requires selective techniques.

Salleyland has at least 26 species of fishes. Techniques to collect them have been varied but not unusual: minnow traps, rod and reel, trashcan traps, seine, dip net, and cane pole. Finding at least one of the 56 species of amphibians and reptiles known to inhabit the property has been more challenging. Most of the 10 kinds of salamanders have been found under a coverboard. Most frogs and toads (also 10 species) were first added to the list of resident fauna because they were calling. Of the 36 species of reptiles, 6 are turtles, and most individuals have been captured in aquatic funnel traps or seen basking on logs or walking overland. All 8 kinds of lizards have been discovered under coverboards or out and about when season and temperature were optimal. The 22 kinds of snakes, a lot for such a small parcel of land, have been discovered in different ways. Many have only been found under a coverboard. Others have been observed basking, swimming, or traveling overland. The more than 100 different birds documented include neotropical migrants stopping by for a visit on their way north or south, as well as some year-round residents. Nearly all have been seen in person, the majority through binoculars, although their first record may have been because some bird-watcher recognized their call.

Identifying the 25 species of terrestrial mammals living at Salleyland required a far different approach. If you want to document what mammals, other than bats, you have on a targeted patch of land, use a wildlife camera. Although I know wild mammals are around us, often watching us day and night, I have seen more on film than I have in person. In fact, for 8 of the species we have recorded on wildlife cameras at Salleyland, we have yet to see any of them on the land. Think about that. Eight medium-size mammals we know are present manage to evade everyone every time. Coyotes and southern flying squirrels cannot keep their mouths shut on some nights, and bobcats have left their signatures in the sand. None of them have allowed themselves to be seen.

One of the more intriguing camera captures was made by Andrew Grosse, who became the South Carolina state herpetologist after Will Dillman. He and Will installed a variation of a box camera trap, an upside-down five-gallon bucket with an opening cut flush to the ground on opposite sides of the bucket. They mounted a wildlife camera to the inside top of the bucket, pointed toward the ground. When any animal—grasshopper, lizard, snake, bird, mammal—passed through one opening and out the other, the camera took a snapshot of the traveler. All those just mentioned have showed up at one time or another.

Box cameras are used in pairs in concert with a drift fence, which is a barrier of three-foot-high aluminum flashing. When coupled with buckets (pitfall traps) embedded in the ground with the opening parallel and flush to the ground, a drift fence is one of the most effective field collecting techniques ever designed for capturing reptiles and amphibians that travel overland. The concept is simple. When pitfall traps are spaced several feet apart alongside a drift fence, an animal encounters the fence while traveling, turns right or left, is guided toward a bucket, and falls into it. For forty years my students and I published scientific papers based on more than a million reptiles and amphibians we had captured with drift fences and pitfall traps.

But pitfall traps have a drawback. They must be checked at least once a day to keep captured animals from becoming dehydrated, eaten by predators, or drowned during rains. Such constant vigilance is not possible at Salleyland because no one is in residence. However, when a box camera is placed at either end of a fifty-foot-long drift fence, the herding function of the fence serves to steer animals through the bucket where they are caught by a camera. Several photographs have let us know we have at least one striped skunk.

Andrew checks the box cameras every two months and sends me photographs of animals of interest. A Carolina wren is a frequent day visitor, presumably to capture the grasshoppers and spiders that show up. Oldfield mice appear at night to eat what the wrens don't catch. Although we have only encountered three coachwhips over the years, the camera proves the big snakes are around in the warm months. We've never seen or smelled a skunk at Salleyland, but photographs left no question that one of the black-and-white-striped carnivores had entered and squeezed through one of the box camera cans. Animals that ought to be obvious can be surprisingly clandestine.

Find a Burrow

Rooney Floyd asked a question I had answered many times. "What are these big holes in the ground?"

We were in the hardwood forest with scattered pine trees on the hillside above the cabin. I told him I suspected the culprits were armadillos. A sandy apron three feet in diameter had been thrown out of each hole. The half dozen holes were thirty to fifty feet from each other. The surrounding woodland floor of last year's oak and hickory leaves had provided an obvious clue that could turn anyone into a wildlife tracker. Trails the width of an armadillo wove through the leaves, occasionally with a divot the size of an armadillo snout. Most of the holes appeared to have been freshly dug so I told Rooney I would set up a wildlife camera to see if one of the perpetrators could be caught in action. It only took one night to identify an adult nine-banded armadillo and four smaller ones coming out of the burrow. Armadillos have genetically identical quadruplets and the same-sex squadron of four stay together for several weeks or months after birth before dispersing across the landscape.

Two nine-banded armadillos emerge from a burrow they dug in a sandy bank a few days earlier. Armadillos have spread from Florida over much of the eastern United States in the last few decades. Photo by author.

Armadillos belong to a distinctive family comprising around twenty species of insect-eating mammals. Most live in Central and South America. Only the nine-banded armadillo is native to the United States. In the 1950s nine-banded armadillos were in Louisiana and Texas and had been introduced into southern Florida, where they had become quite conspicuous by the 1960s. Today, these prehistoric-looking creatures have spread through most of Georgia, Alabama, and Mississippi, on to Tennessee, North Carolina, and Illinois. Questions from suburbanites about how to get rid of armadillos have increased as these armored burrowers have become more abundant. They continue to extend their geographic range.

Armadillos' food comes from beneath the soil, which they dig up with enormous shovel-like front feet as they search for beetle grubs living in the dirt. They also eat hundreds of other kinds of insects and worms. In a natural wooded area, armadillos leave a recognizable trail through the woods with occasional diggings and burrows. Some are deep enough for other animals to use when the armadillo moves on. In suburban communities, part of the armadillo nuisance factor comes from their digging in soft soil—such as raised flower beds, tilled gardens, and watered lawns. In my experience, an armadillo shows up for no apparent reason, roots around in the yard a bit and digs a burrow or two. It seldom stays for long. Eventually it will wander from my yard to a neighbor's and then on to someone else's.

Armadillos are nearsighted, so it is often possible to get close enough to catch one. If you spot an armadillo during daytime, the technique for removing it is simple enough. Chase it down, grab the long tail, lift the animal off the ground. I have never heard of an armadillo biting a person. But they do flail their feet trying to escape, and their sharp claws can deliver a deep scratch. I once took Parker to an urgent care when he was clawed by an armadillo. The wound required ten stitches. He has since learned to avoid the claws by picking the armadillo up by the tail. I do not recommend this as an armadillo-removal technique for the average homeowner.

How many different kinds of animals take advantage of the holes dug by these mammalian earth-movers? That's a wildlife mystery worth investigating someday. The gopher tortoise, a regional terrestrial turtle, digs its signature burrow in sandy soil. A documented feature of gopher tortoise burrows is the astoundingly high number of other animals that use them as safe harbors to escape predators, cold weather, or drought. Armadillos are relatively new (within the past quarter century) invaders to the eastern United States east of the Mississippi River and north of Florida, where they were first reported in the 1940s. I suspect armadillo burrows will eventually be found to contribute to wildlife refuges for other animals as well, and possibly will also be discovered to be safe havens for a high diversity of regional species. The numbers may be even higher than tortoise burrows because most armadillos dig burrows in woodland dirt as well as in sand, whereas most tortoises dig in more open sandy habitats with lower biodiversity.

Armadillos are the only animal besides humans to naturally acquire leprosy. Leprosy, or Hansen's disease, is caused by a type of bacteria closely related to the one that causes tuberculosis. Kim Marie Tolson, a wildlife biologist at the University of Louisiana at Monroe, and her students have captured hundreds of armadillos to assess them for the presence of the leprosy pathogen. Leprosy has been recognized as a human affliction since biblical times, although Tolson thinks many of the references in the Bible were actually to other skin diseases.

Armadillos often live more than ten years, which is an important point. The incubation period for the leprosy bacteria is at least two years, possibly longer, before it is expressed. Being long-lived is a requirement for contracting leprosy. Virtually all reported cases of leprosy in armadillos have been west of the Mississippi River. Leprosy is not prevalent in Florida, where the largest eastern populations occur, nor is it common in the many new areas of the eastern United States that armadillos are moving into. I am pleased to find armadillos as part of the biodiversity at Salleyland. They have much to offer anyone interested in intriguing albeit odd-looking creatures of the woods.

Bring in the Experts

A day with temperatures in the mid-90s did not keep Sean Graham from showing us how to catch Chamberlain's dwarf salamanders in the Salleyland sphagnum swamp, which he declared was one of the best habitats he had ever seen for these tiniest of amphibians. We gently peeled back the bright green sphagnum where they hid, and in 20 minutes captured and released 17. Final score: Sean 8, Parker 6. I only found 3, but probably more than anyone else in the Southeast caught that day.

SALLEYLAND FIELD NOTES, JUNE 15, 2015

FINDING OUT WHAT WE HAD ON THE PROPERTY WAS ACCOMPLISHED IN several ways. I knew a little bit about most of the regional wildlife and had plenty of field guides and other books to assist me. I also knew how little I knew about most of the life that surrounds us in the wild. But I usually knew who did know a lot about particular groups of organisms and was friends or at least colleagues with many of them. By involving professional ecologists and wildlife biologists, botanists, invertebrate zoologists, sandhill specialists, stream biologists, mushroom collectors, and other specialists visiting Salleyland, I could fill in many natural history gaps. Geologists and archaeologists helped round out the story of the land.

Do not doubt that someone can be an expert about a group of organisms, perhaps even the best in the world, without having a formal degree. Experienced and competent amateurs made numerous contributions as we went about learning what shared the land with us. I can hardly think of a species or taxonomic group of animals or plants for which I cannot find someone who knows more than I do. I invited as many of that ilk to Salleyland as I could find. I still do. Anyone can find an expert who knows about various aspects of the wildlife of a park or other prescribed area. Most experts are eager to share what they know with anyone who is interested.

Allison puts the final touches on one of the swamp jumpers,
which give people a boardwalk through the swamp and animals
a coverboard to hide under. Photo by Mike Gibbons.

A visiting herpetology class checks a swamp jumper coverboard
in search of salamanders. Photo by Mike Gibbons.

How to Catch a Bat

"Grandpa, how do you catch a bat?" I considered telling Parker, "I don't." Instead, I said, "I know someone who studies bats. Let's have her show us." The someone was Joy O'Keefe, director of the Center for Bat Research, Outreach, and Conservation at Indiana State University. She was visiting her husband, Mark Vukovich, in our hometown, Aiken, South Carolina, and agreed to demonstrate not only how to catch a bat but also how to find out what bats are flying around that you don't catch. Catching them is not so easy. Mike, Parker, and I found this out within a couple of hours after meeting Joy and Mark at the cabin before dusk.

Joy wanted to record which bats were present and examine them as part of her research. One method of bat inventory is the mist net. Imagine a volleyball net made of thread so thin that a bat's echolocation signals do not bounce back as readily as they do from a solid tree trunk or building. The result—flying bats get tangled in the net. The four nets we set that night ranged from twenty to forty feet long. Bats fly at night by using echolocation, which allows them to find insect prey and to avoid physical structures. But they have tiny eyes and can see in the daytime. They are occasionally active during the day, especially at dusk, so we set up the four sets of nets before dark. Mark, Mike, and Parker were Joy's assistants during this event, carrying poles that the nets were tied to, standing them up, and getting the nets stretched—two across the creek and two in the woods across the road to the cabin. I helped by staying out of the way and taking notes.

When a bat gets caught, the researcher must get to the net and capture the bat before it chews its way free. Every ten minutes beginning at dusk we took turns checking mist nets to see if a bat had been caught. Parker, Joy, and Mark waded waist-deep in cold water to set the mist nets and later to check them. Mike and I kept careful watch from the bridge over the stream. Somebody had to stay dry to take notes.

Of the more than forty-five kinds of bats found in the United States, the eastern red bat and the evening bat are among those present in the Southeast. We caught several of each kind that night and saw how terrifying a bat can look close-up. Mike wondered if perhaps George Lucas got ideas for some of his creepy Star Wars characters from a personal encounter with a bat. Being of an earlier generation, I tried to recall if Bela Lugosi had such vicious-looking fangs in the movie *Dracula*. Meanwhile, Joy, who knows how to handle a bat, took measurements of each one's weight and wing spread and identified its sex.

There is more to bats than just a ferocious face with a mouthful of sharp teeth. Each time Joy released one, we watched as it disappeared into the surrounding night and marveled at one of the most graceful flying creatures imaginable. Eastern red bats are beautiful. Males have a soft, furry, reddish-orange coat. Females are more yellowish. Red bats have a broad tail and big wings that they use like a catcher's mitt to capture moths and beetles in flight.

Evening bats are darker, kind of scary looking, and smell like burnt wood. They too are awesome in flight.

Joy also brought a technological device used in bat research—an Anabat bat detector. When turned on, the device registers the ultrasonic echolocation sounds of bats in the vicinity. The Anabat revealed that three more species were flying around that night although we did not catch any of them. Something to look for in the mist nets the next time Joy pays a visit to Salleyland.

Conservation biologists are concerned about a type of fungus that can grow on the exposed skin of bats and cause death during hibernation. The fungus causes a disease known as white-nose syndrome (WNS). The origin of the fungus is unknown, but it has been found on bats in Europe and Asia. WNS is known to be a cause of population declines in several cave-dwelling bats that hibernate colonially. Part of Joy's research is to determine whether bats in our region are infected. Because the fungus that causes WNS is contagious among bats, she takes great care to wash the nets after each use when the sampling is completed. While taking the measurements that night she wore a new set of gloves for each bat and didn't let observers touch the bats. That part was fine with me.

Set Out Bird Boxes

Over the years we have set out about a dozen each of bird boxes and duck boxes, which we periodically check. The duck boxes have been especially exciting, yielding several clutches of wood ducks. We also discovered one clutch of ten hooded mergansers, thanks to a visit by Andrew Lydeard and John Hewlett from Murray State University. We had spent the night at the cabin. Fortuitously and fortunately we happened to open a duck box early on the morning the mergansers hatched.

I had checked this box periodically for the past six weeks. A new egg was added to the clutch each day. I had never seen the female that was laying the eggs because they do not begin incubating them till the last one is laid. Then they only leave the nest box a time or two each day to feed, spending the rest of their time sitting on the eggs. I had assumed this was a wood duck's nest. In the previous two years a female wood duck had had successful hatches in this box. Fortunately Andrew was there when we opened the box. He is an outstanding ornithologist and immediately recognized the baby ducklings as hooded mergansers, not wood ducks. Turns out no one had reported a hooded merganser in the more than one hundred species of birds that had been recorded at Salleyland up till that day. But there they were. Peeping and ready to leave the nest. Always good to have an expert with you.

In the time it took us to go back to the cabin and bring the others down to see the ducklings, about thirty minutes, they were all gone from the box. We found them puddling around in the water amid tall aquatic vegetation, staying in a tight cluster, and peeping. Were they calling their mother? Where was she? Presumably, she saw us, but we never saw her.

The group of us walked across the bridge and left the area on the far side of the creek where the ducklings were. When we looked back they were following us! Seemingly they had imprinted on us in lieu of their missing mother. Cool behavior to see, but not good for surviving in the Salleyland swamp and stream. We distanced ourselves, leaving the baby ducks at the water's edge in hopes that the mother would return as soon as we were out of sight. I don't know the outcome but hope we eventually have ten more hooded mergansers resident in the area.

We have seen duck eggs in almost every box every year. In one case, a pair of great crested flycatchers nested in a box I watched for a couple weeks from our porch overlooking the stream. But a safe hatching from a duck box at Salleyland is not the norm, to the point that we call them rat snake boxes instead of duck boxes. Ornithological purists who are focused on ensuring success for the nesting bird the box is named after (e.g., bluebird, wood duck) take various preventive measures to guard against boxes becoming open community housing or fast-food outlets for predators. An aluminum baffle encircling a tree or pole can keep raccoons from raiding a nest and squirrels from building one. But no predator guard I know of can keep a six-foot rat snake at bay.

Whether you want to protect a preferred species or take a laissez-faire approach, duck boxes and bluebird boxes offer excellent opportunities to experience wildlife. You'll probably find something inside the box—be prepared to enjoy whatever you find.

Oding Reveals Some Fascinating Creatures

I went oding for the first time in May 2017. If you have never gone looking for odes (other than in a poetry book), you should give it a try. If you learn something about them first or go with a knowledgeable guide, you will not be disappointed. It may be one of the most thrilling nature walks you take.

"Odes" is the colloquial name given to insects in the taxonomic order Odonata, the dragonflies and damselflies. All are carnivorous, specializing on insect prey, so based on some folks' criteria they are beneficial to have around. I asked Peter Stangel if he and any other odonate experts he knew could visit Salleyland to go oding. He invited John Demko and Hilda Flamholtz. All three are remarkable ode trackers. John and Hilda add photographic skills that are humbling.

We met at the cabin and were soon in the woods, alongside the stream, and into the sphagnum swamp. Odonates can be found in diverse places, so we spent time in the field and sandhill habitat with young longleaf pine. The thrill of the hunt soon surfaced and remained with me all day. As with most groups of animals with high species diversity, once you focus on their ecological and behavioral traits, different biopersonalities emerge. Also, as with many taxonomic groups, special tools or techniques may be useful. I was not expecting binoculars to be part of the search kit but soon found out their value. Counting body segments and seeing eye color are often clues to identifying dragonflies. Being able to see key markers without having to approach too closely and alarm a resting odonate is desirable.

Dragonflies are familiar as the four-winged, fast-moving aerial predators that patrol fields and ponds in search of flying insects. When I was a kid in New Orleans, we called them mosquito hawks, which gave them indisputable "beneficial" status. Damselflies, a.k.a. snake doctors, as we called them when I was a kid in Tuscaloosa, are most common in swamps and shaded stream margins. At Salleyland, we saw numerous ebony jewelwings, with their solid black wings, flitting around like fairies in shaded spots. When these dainty damselflies perch in sunlight, the abdomen (the long body extension that looks like a tail) appears metallic green or blue. These are beautiful creatures whose gentle nature should make anyone appreciate the edge of a swamp. With a little coaching, I learned to tell the ebony jewelwing males from the females, which have a white spot on the wing tips.

Odonates cover the color spectrum, with bodies ranging from bright red and orange to yellow, green, blue, and violet. Some may even have invisible-to-us ultraviolet colors on certain body parts. The common whitetail dragonfly, unimaginatively named, as adult males have a distinctive, solid white abdomen, was abundant. In *The Southern Wildlife Watcher*, Rob Simbeck gives a thorough and captivating overview of the intricate behavior and ecology of the species. Eye color often reveals the species of an odonate. We saw dragonflies called eastern pondhawks with huge bright green eyes. A damselfly known as the variable dancer has purple eyes. The attenuated bluet, another damselfly, has solid blue eyes and a recognizable light blue tip on its long, thin abdomen. If odonates reached the size of eagles, they would be the most spectacular and impressive, as well as terrifying, animals in the air.

Collectively, we were able to locate, identify, and even photograph more than thirty different species of dragonflies and damselflies. Some were rare, such as the duckweed firetail, a reddish damselfly that rests on mats of tiny duckweed plants covering some aquatic habitats. Another, the sphagnum sprite, was restricted to an area of sphagnum moss growing deep in the swamp. Some were ones that Peter, John, and Hilda had never seen in this locale; they qualified as new county records. As an untrained initiate in the ode club, I recognized only a few, although I had walked through those fields, woods, and swamps many times.

I was astonished to realize so many kinds of dragonflies and damselflies have been around me unnoticed in these habitats for years. This is true for much of the vibrant array of biodiversity that surrounds us anytime we venture into a natural habitat.

For me, the day of oding was educational and exciting, a fabulous exercise in environmental search and discovery. The same can be true of any nature walk, whether the quest is for odonates, birds, or flowers. Mushrooms, snakes, and lichens make fitting taxonomic search targets as well. Whatever you search for, once you tune in to the diversity of life around us, you become more aware of—and therefore more appreciative of—the natural world. Having a pair of binoculars and an expert or so by your side is also a good idea if you are on ode hunt.

Purseweb Spiders Are Worth the Walk

We turned a walk in the woods into a wildlife adventure without seeing a single live animal over three inches long. We saw some of the usual suspects one might encounter on a casual stroll through a mixed hardwood and pine forest on a sunny day in late fall. We also learned that even the most mundane creatures have a story to tell. Rudy Mancke knows the stories. Rudy is the quintessential champion of the environment, well known for his long-running SCETV show *NatureScene* and his public radio and TV program *NatureNotes*. He reveals the hidden secrets of the natural world to viewers and listeners. Also with us on this walk was Tony Mills, Master Naturalist and award-winning host of the educational TV program *Coastal Kingdom*. I knew with Rudy and Tony on hand, we would find something of interest.

As soon as Rudy arrived at the cabin, he pointed out a bright yellow dot flitting through the brown-leaved forest landscape, first in sunshine then in shadow. The cloudless sulfur was the only butterfly we saw, but as Rudy noted, the sighting was special. Cloudless sulfurs have been reported to hibernate as adults. This one had probably been dormant during the last week of cold weather, only to emerge with the warming trend to brighten up an otherwise drab scene.

Wildlife can be enjoyed year-round if you know what to look for. We captured an insect with long, fragile-looking legs and a needle-shaped body that we learned was a thread-legged bug, an ambush predator. This one preys mainly on what it finds in spiderwebs, a precarious profession. Using its four back legs to walk deftly on the webs without sticking, the thread-legged bug jabs with its front legs to grab its victim, which are trapped insects, or maybe an occasional spider. A spider does not like to see a thread-legged bug in its parlor.

Spiders themselves are formidable carnivores, with jaws that have fangs at the tip. In all but a few cases, the fangs can inject venom while the powerful jaws keep prey from escaping. Many, such as the regal jumping spider, can be safely picked up. Parker correctly identified it. When Rudy pulled out his ever-present magnifying glass, we could see the large front pair of eyes characteristic of jumping spiders. We also saw the silvery coloring around its metallic-looking mouth and learned that it was a male.

The environmental adventure continued, sometimes fueled by questions from the family and sometimes by Rudy himself pointing out an overlooked life-form. I knew we had hit pay dirt when he exclaimed, "This is unbelievable! Do you know what this is?" Fortunately I kept my mouth shut and did not proclaim that it looked like a fungus-covered limb as I marveled at Rudy's enthusiasm. It was the home of a purseweb spider, the first ever reported from the county. An exciting find even for Rudy Mancke.

The web looked like a footlong twig lying against the base of an oak tree. The columnar tube seemed innocuous enough to a casual observer, but inside lived a monster, a relative of the tarantula. Purseweb spiders have huge jaws and fangs that are called into play in an unusual fashion. When a fly or other insect crawls on the column of silk, the spider comes up the tube from belowground and attacks from the inside, biting through the webbing, grabbing the prey, and pulling it inside. Pursewebs can live up to five years, so we marked the spot for future observation.

Tony pointed out a coyote den with the fur of an opossum and part of an armadillo shell outside the entrance. But we had all seen coyotes, opossums, and armadillos—dead and alive. The purseweb spiderweb and thread-legged bug won the Wow! award for that day. Any walk in the woods can be memorable. Just remember to carry a magnifying glass with you.

Six Big Cats Once Lived at Salleyland

A chipped flint or burnt stone reminds us that people lived here thousands of years ago. A sweetgum with a long-healed scar of stripped bark tells of beavers. One day we discovered a more recent past—a bobcat's paw print in the sand.

Scott Pfaff pointed it out as Will Dillman, Steve Bennett, and I took turns applauding each other for noticing deer tracks of different sizes heading in different directions. We all found the bobcat track more intriguing. Predators are usually more exciting than prey. Bobcats, the only relatively common though seldom seen native cat in North America, can weigh more than forty pounds. The bobcat's northern counterpart, the Canada lynx, is a bit larger. The two "big cats" living today in the Western Hemisphere are the mountain lion (a.k.a. panther, cougar, puma) and the jaguar. Much less common than bobcats, mountain lions can weigh more than two hundred pounds; jaguars, more than three hundred. Impressive? How would you feel about sharing your neighborhood with cats weighing six, seven, or eight hundred pounds? As Scott noted, they once lived right where we were musing about the signature in the sand left by the previous night's bobcat.

Scott knows a lot about big cats. According to him, six of these giants were prowling around the Southeast a few thousand years ago looking for prey, mostly large hoofed animals. Presumably, this was not a good time for humans to be wandering around in the forest alone. The earliest inhabitants of North America probably crossed paths with several big cats that are no longer with us. The paw print at our feet might have been several inches across if any were still around.

Paleontologists, even armed with modern tools for DNA analysis, do not agree about the evolutionary origins of and relationships between many of the North American big cats. Some hypotheses suggest they are descendants of ancient European, Asian, or African species. Of the two still with us, jaguars are mostly in Central and South America, but individuals occasionally enter some of the southwestern states near the Mexican border. Mountain lions are still present in the states west of the Mississippi River, but outside of southern Florida, no populations have been verified in the East, although individual sightings are often reported. The other four are all extinct, but fossil material provides confirmation of their existence.

The best-known extinct big cat was *Smilodon*, the so-called saber-toothed tiger, although true tigers are not known to have ventured south of Alaska. Everyone has seen drawings of saber-tooths with their incisors extending from the front of the upper jaw. The longest *Smilodon* teeth were more than ten inches. Upon encountering saber-tooths, the first humans to arrive on the continent probably wondered whether the trip across the Bering Strait from Siberia had been a good idea. The eventual extinction of these big cats with the remarkable teeth occurred about ten thousand years ago and was no doubt a relief to all edible inhabitants, including early humans.

Another species, the scimitar-toothed cats, are known scientifically as *Homotherium*. Their front canine teeth were shorter than those of *Smilodon*, but they were massive enough and sharp enough to bring down a woolly mammoth. The scimitar-toothed cats were as large as an African lion. The American lion was even larger, with adults having an average weight of more than a quarter of a ton. One was estimated to have weighed more than seven

Experts from many scientific disciplines, including biology, geology, and chemistry, visit Salleyland. This photo includes three state herpetologists and three university ecologists. Photo by Stephen Bennett.

hundred pounds. The sixth big cat, the American cheetah, was presumably like the modern cheetah of Africa in being able to outrun fast prey, even pronghorn antelope of the western plains.

Reasons for the decline and disappearance of America's big cats are speculative at best. Did competition with humans lead to their demise? I doubt that early hunters with their primitive spears could have been the direct cause of extinction for any of these cats. Mountain lions are now virtually gone from the eastern United States, but even that took a couple of centuries of relentless pursuit by men with dogs and guns. A more likely explanation is that the big cats of the past gradually died out with the decline of the large prey they depended on for food. Speculation continues among paleontologists about what happened to the camels, horses, and mammoths of North America.

At Salleyland we might encounter a bobcat almost anywhere. At the very least we can look forward to finding a print in the sand or getting a wildlife camera photo that assures us of its presence.

How Do You Find a Blue Ghost?

The Blue Ghost. A specter in a folk tale? A villain in an old Western? No. It's a firefly (a.k.a. lightning bug) that emits a bluish-green light instead of the classic yellow associated with backyard lightning bugs. Blue ghost males fly low to the ground, creating an eerie night scene in the woods. The wingless females are on the ground, emitting a glow from tiny portholes on a worm-like body. Some males shine a tiny spotlight like a police helicopter's as they fly over the ground in search of females.

I was with two experts. One, Joe Mitchell, a herpetologist, was of no more help than I in searching for a mysterious firefly. The other, Lynn Faust, is an international authority on these bioluminescent beetles.

Blue ghosts, which occur in the southern Appalachians, appear in early spring. None had been found where we were, more than a hundred miles to the south. Lynn was on a quest to determine whether they were present at Salleyland. We might not find any blue ghosts, but with an expert to identify whatever fireflies we did find, our nocturnal mission would not be a failure.

Setting out around sunset, we walked for three hours through woods, along the edge of a swamp, and beside a deserted road. Our quarry had its own light. Fireflies depend on their blinking lights for communication between males and females. We did not want to distract them with a handheld source of light pollution. We wanted them to go about their nighttime business undisturbed by us. Walking in the dark can be an exhilarating experience in itself. If we had turned on a light or opened a cell phone, our eyes would have needed several minutes to readjust to the dark.

Our first firefly sighting came at dusk—white flashes high in the trees as we overlooked the swamp. The species is known as the spring treetop flasher, an apt if unimaginative name. In most of the eastern United States, the spring treetop flasher is the first flashing firefly seen each year. Earlier, trying to be the first to spot the firefly after Lynn told us what to look for, I had pointed at a light moving above the swamp through the night sky. Lynn and Joe both politely noted that those were the lights of an airplane. A few minutes later the tops of the trees along the swamp margin were twinkling with the real thing. In *Fireflies, Glow-worms, and Lightning Bugs* Lynn discusses how color perception of some firefly lights can change. As we age, the flashing lights of the spring treetop flasher may appear to be white. Most younger people see yellow. The lights in the swamp looked white to me.

Spring treetop flashers mate on tree trunks and lay their eggs on them. They are often visible as high-flying lights in the trees in early spring. We saw dozens that night, most near the tops of tall pines and hardwoods. That was the only firefly we saw in the air. Each species has a signature pattern of flashing that can be used for identification. Later in the spring, other species will appear, most glowing much lower to the ground. In late May we watch for the synchronous fireflies. Thousands light up the woods at once and then go dark for a few seconds, a phenomenon we have seen at Salleyland.

To find most wild animals, you have to be in the right place, during the right season, on the right day, at the right time. With the blue ghosts, the flying males are blinking during a short window of only about fifteen minutes shortly after dusk. At least one of these provisos, and maybe more, was wrong for the blue ghost firefly, as we did not find one that night. But Lynn is confident that the place is right; therefore, so am I. Once the season is right, I will just need to find the right night and be sitting in the dark at the right time. I plan to look for them every year until we find them, because a walk through dark woods and swamps in search of a ghostly light promises to be an environmental adventure of its own.

Plant Inventory

When I was a student at the University of Alabama decades ago, I took a course in plant taxonomy from Joab Thomas, an outstanding botanist who was a member of the biology department. Over the years, as I focused more on vertebrate ecology, my limited plant identification skills began to fade like autumn leaves on a maple tree. I was going to need some expert help at Salleyland. For me to complete a plant inventory, the expert needed to be a botanist.

On the whole, most people are more interested superficially in animals than in plants, partly because the former tend to be action figures whereas plants are mostly inert unless the wind is blowing. But intriguing plants abound if you know enough about them. Most plants could do well if no animals existed, but few animals can exist without plants. A bobcat ultimately depends on plants to survive because the rat or rabbit it catches for food makes its living eating some form of vegetation. The complex food web depends on plant life as its base. I wanted to add plants to my species list for Salleyland as all plants serve as superb examples of the diversity of life and hold many secrets and mysteries that await our understanding. I made headway in identifying some trees, shrubs, and aquatic vegetation through the use of field guides and by asking visiting colleagues who were botanists about ones of interest, but I still did not have a comprehensive list of plants on the property.

I solved the problem of setting a baseline for plant identification when Rooney Floyd brought Patrick McMillan, who was then professor of environmental sustainability at Clemson University and director of the South Carolina Botanical Garden, to spend a day at Salleyland. Patrick wanted to bring along a clipboard and pencil to write down the names of all the plants we saw. I thought he might wind up with a list of a few dozen trees, shrubs, and anything flowering on that spring day. But no. When we returned to the cabin after a three-hour field trip through a variety of habitats, I was astounded. He had identified 236 different plant species! Many of them were grasses, sedges, and forbs that were complete unknowns to me.

Any skepticism about whether Patrick got them right dwindled to near zero as other visiting botanists confirmed the identifications. And only a few have reported a species he did not have on his list (probably because I did not take him to the proper location or microhabitat). I have learned more than I have taught about wildlife and natural history at Salleyland because of the many visitors who clearly know more than I about various taxonomic groups. With Patrick I hoped to at least excel in the area of herpetology on our walk through the woods and swamp. That hope was soon dashed. I was leading the way toward some coverboards I knew would have salamanders under them when I realized Patrick had stopped. I looked back to see him pointing, clearly amused, at a big black racer. I had stepped right over it without seeing it.

One of the more exciting discoveries that day was a beautiful little plant with pink flowers that grows beside the road to the cabin. I had seen them every year, not realizing there was anything special about them. Patrick declared that the wild pinks blooming along SNAP Road and up into the woods was the largest population he had ever seen. More confirmation of just how special Salleyland is. Faunal and floral inventories on any land you have access to can contribute to your fuller enjoyment of the natural biodiversity that surrounds you. Bringing a botanist along to find plants and snakes can be useful in building your species list.

Don't Let Mushrooms Intimidate You

I have always been intimidated by mushrooms. Not scared of them. Not repulsed by them. Simply daunted by how many different kinds there are and disheartened by my own ignorance regarding them. Now, having invited a mycologist (someone who studies fungi) to Salleyland to instruct me and suggest a field guide for reference, I'm feeling more confident.

Two days after a rain, always a good time for mushrooms, I asked Tess Moody to visit our woods and show us some of the different fungi sprouting up here and there. We picked and photographed dozens of mushrooms, some of which I had never seen because they were too small, too hidden, or too camouflaged for the inexperienced eye. The next day she sent an email. "I have identified 39 species so far, but I will have more!" I was encouraged. Maybe I would be able to put names to the red, white, and blue mushrooms I had seen all my life, in addition to some of the yellow, green, and purple ones. Maybe black and brown ones would also be identified.

Tess found tiny mushrooms called yellow fairy cups that I would almost certainly have overlooked. She pointed out identifying traits and ecological attributes of everything we found. She suggested I consult the field guide *Mushrooms of the Southeast* by Todd F. Elliott and Steven L. Stephenson. The assertion that "the Southeast is one of the most mycologically diverse regions in the world" explains why so many mushrooms inhabited the Alabama woods where I grew up and were common in neighboring states. Scientists estimate that more than 5 million species of fungi live on Earth. Of these, only 100,000 have been identified and named. In addition to mushrooms, the fungus world includes molds and yeasts.

The fact that only 2 percent of the world's fungi have been described does not mean that all those toadstools growing in wet woods and suburban yards haven't been named. They have. But most fungi are microscopic, and the majority of those have never been seen by a human. The traditional mushroom everyone is familiar with is the "fruiting body of any fungus able to be observed in the field." Though representing only a small subset of the fungi of the world, each has a part to play in its own ecosystem. Many serve the important environmental role of decomposing dead plants. Some, such as the penicillin mold, have been co-opted for their medical value to humans. Who knows how many species yet to be discovered might prove equally beneficial. Perhaps another penicillin capable of curing a common ailment is right beneath our feet. Another reason for not destroying biodiversity we know nothing about.

During our visit to the woods, Tess pointed out some mushrooms distinctive enough to be identified on sight. The earthstar has indentations around the cap that look like rays radiating from the center. We found several jelly fungi growing on fallen trees. They look and feel like Jell-O and come in a variety of colors, including snow white. The wood ear jelly fungus looks disturbingly like human ears clustered together. I did not ask if they were edible because it would have made no difference to me.

Tess showed us how to tell a turkey tail mushroom from a false turkey tail mushroom. They both grow on dead trees like a series of semicircular plates adjacent to or overlapping others of its kind. Each has concentric rings, resembling the fanned-out tail of a turkey, but a simple technique can separate the true from the false. The turkey tail has pores visible on the underside, giving it a rough feel. The false turkey tail is smooth.

On the back porch I had what I thought was a turkey tail mushroom I had picked up a few days before. Tess showed me another way to tell it was a false turkey tail. She told me to put it in my mouth for a moment. Trusting her not to let me ingest a poisonous mushroom, I did. It turned red! A turkey tail will not do that. I try to keep one of each on the back porch now to show visitors. The more daring agree to hold one in their mouth. Others prefer to pour water on it. One mystery remains. Why does the false turkey tail turn red?

New discoveries continued throughout the day, many requiring a hand lens. Tess took home several mushrooms to create spore prints (a diagnostic technique to identify certain mushrooms) and to consult online taxonomic keys to confirm identifications. Though I still have a lot to learn about fungi, thanks to Tess and *Mushrooms of the Southeast* I am no longer cowed by their sheer diversity. The field guide authors discuss more than a half dozen categories of mushroom toxins, making the point that some closely related mushrooms have both edible and poisonous species. An admonition given on the first page of the book cannot be overstated. "Eating wild mushrooms is inherently risky. Mushrooms can be easily mistaken, and individuals vary in their physiological reactions to mushrooms that are touched or consumed."

I once heard someone ask a college professor teaching a class on mushrooms, if we could eat a particular mushroom we had found in the forest. He gave the classic response: "You can eat any mushroom once." I don't know who first said that, but I know where I stand on the issue. I am not the least bit concerned about the possibility of ingesting a poisonous mushroom. I don't do my mushroom shopping alone in the woods and never will. But you need not identify every plant, animal, and fungus you find in the woods to enjoy the encounter.

Delve into Wildlife Mysteries

Parker and Nick found a freshly dead, very large banded water-snake on SNAP Road. It was missing its head. They left it in the road but cleared the sand around it so we could see any tracks if something got it. When we went to look at the snake an hour later, it was gone! No tracks visible. Did a large bird (hawk, crow, great blue heron) get it? Two major mysteries. What killed the snake and took only its head? Where did the body go after the boys left it?

SALLEYLAND FIELD NOTES, NOVEMBER 8, 2014

A COLLATERAL FEATURE OF LOOKING FOR AND OBSERVING REPTILES and amphibians has always been discovering other organisms. Native rodents build nests and nurse babies beneath coverboards. Small fish and aquatic insects enter minnow traps. Colorful mushrooms and small ground-dwelling flowering plants live in all woodland habitats. But in the past my targets had been particular herpetofaunal residents for one research goal or another. The by-products—fungi, plants, and other animals—were of passing interest but seldom pursued intellectually in their own right. I had learned the names of some and what their general ecology was by listening to colleagues in other fields. I found out more about some of them by reading field guides. But when I was conducting ecological research as a fulltime professional, staying on task about the study in progress ruled the day. Finding out about other life-forms was a secondary pleasure. Not so when you are retired. The natural world is endlessly fascinating and constantly changing and you can delve into anything that interests you.

Why Do Some Animals Glow in the Dark?

When we turned our flashlights off at midnight, the gibbous moon was waning. Where we stood, in the middle of the pine and mixed-hardwood forest above the cabin, moonlight was sparse. I wanted to show Tess Moody and Parker a creature that glowed in the dark, and the near-black terrain would prove to be an advantage instead of a hindrance. Showing Tess a southeastern animal with which she is not already familiar is hard to do. And Parker had encountered most of the animals at Salleyland. Nonetheless I thought I might soon edify them both. "I have no idea if we'll find one, but let's give it a try." We turned on our handheld ultraviolet blacklights, which emitted a purple glow, not a beam of white light. We were going to look for millipedes.

Some of the large cherry millipedes at Salleyland can be found under logs during the day. An overland traveler is most likely to be found at night. Finding one with a regular flashlight is possible, but a UV light greatly increases your chances during the early spring.

The first few minutes of bumbling around in the dark with only a purple light for illumination were disconcerting, and we saw nothing that didn't look purple. Then Tess held her light on a spot a hundred feet away. We all began moving toward the eerie blue glow on the forest floor. I was elated because I had only seen this phenomenon twice before. My most recent experience had been in the Sonoran Desert with Randy Babb, a naturalist with the Arizona Game and Fish Department, who had taken Mike, Parker, and me to find scorpions with a UV light.

The explanation for why scorpions glow in the dark when you shine a UV light on them is not completely understood. Scorpions have hard shells like crawfish, and the fluorescent property is in the shell or cuticle. When scorpions shed their skin, which they do periodically, they do not glow until the cuticle grows back. The persistence of the fluorescent molecules is measured not in days or even years. Scorpions preserved for decades in museums continue to glow. A few fossil scorpions millions of years old reveal glowing cuticles under a UV light. The short wavelength UV light is invisible to humans, but when it reflects off fluorescent molecules it assumes a longer wavelength we are able to see. Salleyland has no scorpions, so we set out to find millipedes. As I had discovered many years before, they also glow in the dark.

Kurt Buhlmann and I had been using blacklights along the wooded margin of a wetland as we looked for glowing specks of fluorescent powder he had placed on baby turtles during a field experiment. The powder gradually rubs off as the turtles move through the leaf litter allowing us to follow their shining trails. Kurt and I were surprised when we saw a greenish-blue glow on the forest floor. Much larger than any of the powder flecks we were tracking, it turned out to be a cherry millipede, more than two inches long, ambling across the forest floor. It glowed like a scorpion in UV light.

Tess's discovery of a millipede at Salleyland thrilled all of us. We picked up the bright red-and-black cherry millipede, which emits a sweet smell reminiscent of maraschino cherries. The secretion is a chemical compound comparable to hydrogen cyanide, making them poisonous to most would-be predators and probably deadly to some. Millipedes are harmless to handle if the secretions do not get into open cuts or your eyes. One of the red-banded millipedes is a delightful find because of their aromatic scent. Smelling them is okay. Tasting them is not.

The colorful cherry millipedes should not be confused with the bright red centipedes. They are also local woodland residents, but they have fangs that inject venom. The Salleyland centipedes are predatory on woodland invertebrates; millipedes make a living eating plant material and scavenging in rotting wood. Millipedes and centipedes both have lots of legs. Distinguishing one from the other is easy enough: millipedes have two pairs of legs per body segment whereas centipedes have only one. A drawback to this biological clue of course is that if you pick up a centipede, you'll be grabbed by its front pair of pincers and envenomated. No need to count legs; you will already know what you picked up.

We continued our purple-forest-floor search for thirty minutes and found another millipede, a brown-and-yellow one in the same family, by spotting the blue glow. What makes them reflect UV light in this manner? Is it the same optical physics as scorpions? Do other millepedes glow in the dark? None of us knew. But not knowing the answer should never detract from the enjoyment of a wildlife experience. During the last few minutes of our nighttime field trip we found several rotting stumps with hundreds of flecks of bright green, glowing organisms. Were these slime molds? This poorly understood group of organisms, once thought to be fungi, are now considered a biological kingdom of their own. Do millipeds glow because they eat slime molds and incorporate their luminescent cells into their own bodies? More unanswered questions. Biological mysteries abound and remain unsolved until the right person decides to investigate. The first step, of course, is to be aware that a phenomenon exists.

Special lighting has revealed that many animals display colors otherwise invisible to the naked eye. A study by Jennifer Y. Lamb and Matthew P. Davis of Saint Cloud State University in Minnesota published online by *Nature* revealed that body parts of some salamanders reflect colors when illuminated by a blue light. Many are naturally colorful creatures already.

Whether glowing in response to UV light has a purpose for scorpions, millipedes, or anything else is unclear, although scientists always enjoy speculating. Hypotheses include dispelling or confusing predators, protecting the animal from sunlight, and serving as some kind of signal to others of its kind. Or maybe it is just something our technology has revealed and it serves no purpose. Whatever the biological function of fluorescent properties, if there is one, it has nothing to do with people.

We interpret the natural world around us based on what we can perceive. UV technology has unveiled properties not apparent to the naked eye. Discovering what a UV flashlight can reveal is just one more reminder that we still have much to discover about life on Earth.

Oak Trees All in a Row

Why were four enormous southern red oak trees surrounded by much smaller ones set about twenty feet apart in an almost perfect straight line? I had an explanation that was turned on its head when I told an expert about it.

I pointed out the alignment of the trees to Nicolette Cagle, a faculty member at Duke University's Nicholas School of the Environment. My guess had been that a large oak had fallen years ago, and limbs growing up from the trunk had eventually produced roots and continued to grow when the parent tree rotted away. I couldn't have been more wrong.

Nicolette suggested a more likely possibility. The line of trees was the product of an old fencerow. Oak trees do not typically regenerate from a fallen trunk. These oak trees were probably already in a line when they were young ones in a forest of numerous small, randomly spaced trees long ago. Someone building a fence selected those in a relatively straight line so a strand of barbed wire could be wrapped around each to serve as a fence post. When other trees in the area were cleared to form a pasture or agricultural field, they would be the only ones left standing, eventually becoming a line of large trees with barbed wire connecting them.

As Nicolette explained, "Lines of trees typically are planted by people, develop along fencerows, or both." Fruit from trees such as black cherry, red cedar, and hackberry are eaten by birds and often sprout along fence lines. Birds sit on the fence and their droppings contain seeds, which results in new trees. Many seeds go through the digestive system of a bird unharmed. In other bird-tree relationships, the digestion process involves scarification in which the seed coat is broken down, allowing the seed to germinate more easily. New trees are subsequently redistributed across the landscape because the seeds are more successful. In some symbiotic relationships, the bird gets a meal from the fruit surrounding the seed and the tree is propagated in other areas. Birds do not eat and distribute acorns in this manner, so birds were not the answer to the line of oak trees.

As we stood looking at the trees, Nicolette pointed out a malformation in one of them. Philip Schulte, a grad student from Auburn University who was with us, took a closer look and noticed a small strand of barbed wire protruding from the trunk. The wire stuck out a few inches on two sides of the oak tree. Someone else held up a sliver of barbed wire protruding from the side of one of the other trees, lending support to the fence line hypothesis. Nicolette pointed out that barbed wire can be dated based on its design and how it has been used, such as confining livestock, separating property lines, or deterring trespassers.

She took a strand from the tree to estimate its age. The barbed wire seemed "consistent with specimens from the late 1870s or 1880s." Does this mean the fence was strung through the forest before 1900? Possibly. But the wire might have been manufactured years before it was used. My next step in forensic ecology is to have a botanist core the trees. If they turn out to be more than a century old, that will provide support for the theory that a barbed wire fence was erected using little oak trees for fence posts.

Ecological mysteries are all around us. They can make a walk in the woods intriguing. Trying to explain them can be an enjoyable exercise. Keep your mind open to solutions other people suggest that vary from your own, especially if you have an expert who actually knows the answer.

Caterpillars Are Outstanding Teachers

The caterpillars at Salleyland reminded me of two valuable lessons about watching wildlife. You may know nothing about the ecology, behavior, or any other aspect of an organism but still enjoy the encounter. The second lesson is first impressions can be misleading, which is true not just for moths.

I already knew I knew almost nothing about caterpillars except that they turn into moths or butterflies and that someone who studies them is a lepidopterist. I learned the second lesson when we came upon a caterpillar known as the greenstriped mapleworm, a bland looking critter. With help from field guides and lepidopterist friends I realized I had seen the adult form, the rosy maple moth, many times in our fields. Pink and yellow, with a furry look, these daytime moths add color to the browning landscape of late autumn. The caterpillars dine on the leaves of the abundant red maple trees that margin the swamp; the adults do not eat anything. As with so many other insects, the mating behavior of rosy maple moths is not thoroughly understood, but the activities of adults presumably have something to do with reproduction. What else would they have to do? Autumn is the time to look for caterpillars, and I enjoy finding them, whether I can identify them on sight or (more likely) not. I always take a photograph. And using excellent field guides such as David L. Wagner's *Caterpillars of Eastern North America* and reliable internet sources, I am often able to narrow down identification on my own, as was true of the first imperial moth caterpillar we found. I was with Judy Greene and Ken McLeod, friends and former colleagues. We all admired what was clearly a caterpillar worth knowing, although identification came after we returned to the cabin. Imperial moths lay their eggs on a variety of plants for the caterpillars to feed on. Several are found at Salleyland, including oaks, sweetgums, and sassafras. Ken is a botanist and readily identified the plant it was on as a type of viburnum.

Many lepidopterans, including imperial moths, go through several visible changes between the egg laid on a leaf and the adult emerging from a moth cocoon or butterfly chrysalis. The caterpillar we found was a fifth instar—cinnamon-orange colored, showy, altogether impressive, as big around as my thumb and as long as my index finger. Formidable looking spikes ran the length of its body, and bright yellow spots resembling portholes could be seen on its sides.

We admired the huge caterpillar in its gaudy costume as it crawled onto my hand. It would soon weave a cocoon, enter the pupal stage underground, and later turn into a magnificent yellow-and-purple imperial moth, a member of the silkworm family. Why was this one reddish instead of green like some of them? Why do they have little hornlike protuberances on the head? What is the function of the yellow spots? You don't need to understand the biology of a plant or animal to marvel at its wonders.

Like frogs and toads, moths and butterflies lead double lives. Tadpoles and caterpillars are dramatically different in appearance, feeding habits, and other aspects of their ecology from their adult forms. And scientists are a long way from understanding all the factors involved in the transitions. The ecology of some, perhaps most, insects is complicated. Clearly, they have many secrets to reveal, and their small size makes certain observations difficult. The wide variety of caterpillar shapes, colors, and ornamentation reinforces the idea that their ecology and behavior are highly complex. As we continue to uncover intricate ecological strategies in something as seemingly simple as a moth, we realize how much we have to learn.

I looked through my field notes to remind myself about experiences I had had with caterpillars. One Halloween day, John Byrd and I discovered a line of more than thirty caterpillars on a large greenbrier vine at the edge of the swamp. John identified them as caterpillars of the turbulent phosphila moth.

The adults are about as nondescript in appearance as you can imagine—small, brown, bordering on boring. But the caterpillars know how to put on a show. As we watched, several of them raised their black heads with bright white spots. But wait. Is that the head or the tail? When we waved a hand toward the cluster, several heads waved upward toward us. Hold on. Or are those tails wagging up from the mass of bodies and not heads? Yes. Are they reacting to a perceived threat by lifting their tails (which look like the more vulnerable heads) as a defensive lure response to a hungry insect, bird, or maybe a parasitoid wasp? More questions awaiting answers.

Caterpillars can appear in spring as well as autumn. We have found the magnificent giant leopard moth in two different years. We saw one making its way across our dirt road one March; we found another under a coverboard the next April. Both the caterpillar and the adult moth are worthy finds. When the big woolly-bear-like caterpillars roll into a ball, bristly hairs stick out in all directions and bright red bands encircle the body. Presumably, most predators would not have to debate long to decide such a mass of hackles would not be very appetizing. They might also consider the red bands as a warning. Turns out giant leopard moth caterpillars are completely harmless. The moths themselves are not colorful but they are definitely eye-catching. Their large white wings sport shiny black circles, squares, and other geometric markings. An orange abdomen with blue patches provides all the color needed to make a strikingly beautiful animal.

Record your encounters with caterpillars along with other wildlife. You will compile a fascinating saga that will continue every year. Sometimes you will make new discoveries; sometimes you will encounter old friends. With greater understanding of ecosystems and their interconnecting parts, we learn to appreciate our natural environments. And the really pressing questions remain: Why are some imperial moth caterpillars cinnamon orange instead of green? Why do they have little hornlike protuberances on the head? And what on earth is the purpose of those yellow portholes, other than to look pretty?

A Beaver Could Test Your Environmental Conscience

A walk in the woods near our stream gave me the opportunity to witness one of nature's marvels that I had never seen before—the building of a beaver dam. My first evidence of something unusual happening came in autumn after a month of no rain when I measured the water level of the creek. I do this at least once a week downstream from our cabin and was surprised to find that instead of dropping an inch or so, it had actually risen two inches. I attributed it to mismeasurement, until I took my walk.

Beavers are unquestionably keystone species in a region with small to moderate-size streams. They can not only modify the habitat but also change the environment in ways that dramatically influence the lives of plants and animals, including people. Beaver activity can result in big trees dying from flooding and smaller ones being debarked for food or cut down for dam construction. A mile downstream from my incipient beaver dam a larger one has flooded several acres, leaving tall, dead sweetgum and pine trees that began life in a terrestrial habitat and cannot persist in an aquatic one.

Animals are affected, too. Large aquatic salamanders called sirens thrive and become more abundant in pools of a stream created by beaver dams. We once observed more than five hundred sirens along the margins of a small stream when a dam was removed and the water level dropped. Cottonmouths, watersnakes, and turtles are more apparent, maybe even more abundant, around beaver dams, which create areas for basking on sunny days. Waterfowl, such as wood ducks, are attracted to the pond created above the dam. Clearly, beavers and their dams set the tone of the neighborhood for many wildlife species.

The historical geographic range of these gigantic rodents is vast, extending from northern Florida and Mexico to Alaska and Newfoundland. Adult beavers can weigh more than eighty pounds. Their North American ancestors were even bigger, reaching the size of a full-grown black bear. Beavers live thirty-five to fifty years in zoos and more than twenty years in the wild.

The longest beaver dams, reported from Montana and from Alberta, Canada, are over two thousand feet long. Surely beavers across the continent are working feverishly to break the record. Beavers at Salleyland are usually nocturnal. You can see them without the aid of a flashlight only at dusk, when their nighttime activity begins. I have seen one during the day, on top or our beaver dam. Perhaps an OSHA dam safety inspector? I have not yet received a satisfactory answer to this question: why, with few exceptions, do beavers at Salleyland and many other places come out only at night?

For people, one of the conundrums with beavers is that their positive traits—being cute, chubby, and synonymous with industriousness—aren't always enough to outweigh less desirable traits. I know folks who have had beavers cut down a beautiful flowering dogwood tree, flood an area intended for a garden not a fishpond, and dismantle a wooden boathouse to build the beaver lodge. How do you keep beavers for outdoor show-and-tell yet not have them misbehave, from a human's point of view?

An ecofriendly society will always face perplexing wildlife problems and environmental dilemmas. Entertaining, yet potentially destructive, beavers are a good example of the complexity inherent in environmental preservation, with no simple solution as to how to handle the issue. A range of responses are available for dealing with nuisance wildlife. Which solution people choose will depend in part on their environmental conscience.

Too much beaver-dam building on our stream will make it more difficult to navigate up and down in a canoe or Jon boat. But carrying a small boat around the end of a beaver dam to get to the other side of the stream will not be much of an imposition in return for getting to experience a natural phenomenon that can change the character of the habitat and its wildlife. That is, as long as I don't see part of our cabin being used to build that dam.

Natural Historians Make Unusual Discoveries

Parker and I were sitting on the back porch of our cabin across the blackwater stream bordering the sphagnum swamp. A half-mile-wide canopy of trees creates a dark, some might say gloomy, habitat of small pools and rivulets where raccoons, cottonmouths, and bobcats thrive. We were listening to the night sounds of summer, mainly katydids and tree crickets with an occasional raucous dispute between barred owls. Then we heard a sound from deep in the swamp that made us both perk up. A soft, plaintive "woohoo" lasted about a second. Spooky. We looked at each other and each raised an index finger, the universal sign for "be quiet and listen."

We waited and a minute later heard it again. And again. At approximately one-minute intervals the mystery sound was repeated for more than an hour. It clearly was not an insect or frog, so we concluded it must be a bird or mammal. It was no call I had ever heard before that night. We debated whether spending the night at the cabin was a good idea with such an eerie-sounding creature nearby but decided we would be fine.

Earlier that week I had heard the snort of what I thought was a nearby deer while I was standing alone in the swamp with my flashlight off, waiting to see lightning bugs. A moment later a musky smell pervaded the area and I heard rustling vegetation. Disconcerting, to be sure. The sound we heard from the porch was far different. Fortunately, I was able to record both sounds with my phone. Friends familiar with deer later confirmed the snort. I was confident that the new sound would be readily recognized by someone as well, so I set about sending the recording to colleagues who are wildlife biologists or ornithologists What was that call of the wild?

Despite my playing the sound for a dozen colleagues familiar with bird calls and mammal sounds, no one could do more than guess. A mourning dove? But they do not typically call late at night. And why would one want to attract a predator? A chuck-wills-widow or whip-poor-will? We all knew what they sound like, so, no. A fox or coyote? Aside from a barking dog, no regional mammal was known to call continually as a single individual in such a systematic manner.

The possibilities for natural history observations are endless, and wild animals do many things that humans have not observed. Nor do you have to be a professional research ecologist to make an observation that few people have made before. If you are lucky, you'll eventually run across someone who can explain to you what you saw, smelled, or heard.

Months later we got the answer to our mystery sound. I had kept the recording and would play it when I was with someone who had lots of experience with natural phenomena. So, when two members of SCAN (South Carolina Association of Naturalists) were visiting, I gave it another try. We were sitting on the same porch where Parker and I had been when I pulled out my phone to see if they recognized the sound. Their collective response was startling. Simultaneously, they said, "Baby barred owl calling its mother!" They looked at each other in surprise. They had never discussed having heard the sound, yet they had given the exact same answer.

I asked my visitors how they were able to recognize the sound. Gordon Murphy said, "Many years ago I was sitting in the woods, waiting for the sun to come up to do some early morning birding and heard this noise I couldn't identify. I finally got a good look and saw it was a juvenile barred owl." Greg Ross had a similar experience when he observed a family of barred owls in front of his house. He watched "the juveniles interacting with their parents until they matured." Gordon and Greg agreed that they will never forget the sound of a young barred owl calling its mother. Neither will Parker and I.

How Do Pirate Perches Become Invisible?

Ecological mysteries abound, and any animal or plant you encounter has some intrigue in its life. A prime example is a small, unprepossessing freshwater fish called a pirate perch. The black to dark purplish adults, usually less than five inches long, are active at night. Although the fish are common and widely distributed along the Atlantic and Gulf coastal plains and up the Mississippi River valley to the Great Lakes, most people, even seasoned anglers, seldom see one. The fish's preference for weedy waters thick with root masses or floodplain swamps of streams and rivers adds to its inaccessibility. My grandsons and I catch them in minnow traps, small mesh cylinders with inward-pointing funnels at both ends, we set in a swamp.

We like to show pirate perches to visitors. Knowing the name of a plant or animal is the first step in identifying it and talking with others about it. Finding out about its lifestyle, its behavior, and any unusual facts bring the presentation to the next level. Turns out the pirate perch's catchy name is somewhat of a misnomer for two reasons. First, it is not a true perch. It is the only living member of its own family, its close relatives being cave fishes. The other part of its name resulted from an 1872 observation that they do not play well with other small fish when kept in an aquarium. Because of their aggressive behavior, which results in their often being the lone survivor, early ichthyologists dubbed them pirate perches. More modern research has shown their primary prey in the wild to be aquatic invertebrates, although they will eat fish as well as amphibian eggs and larvae. Nonetheless, if you put one in your home aquarium, it will apparently have no qualms about attacking smaller fish—to eat them, of course, not to take their money and jewels.

I was pretty sure of the identity of the first pirate perch Parker, Nick, and Sam caught and hoped I was right. Pirate perches have a bizarre anatomical trait involving the adult anatomy. As with other fishes, reproductive products (eggs and sperm) and body wastes are released through the vent (cloaca), which is usually situated under the body near the tail. The vent is in this location in juvenile pirate perches, but as a pirate perch approaches adulthood, something strange happens. The opening gradually migrates along the underside of the fish until it is positioned under the throat, just behind the gills.

I already knew about their odd anatomy from an ichthyology class I took decades ago. But I had no idea what the functional significance of this arrangement was nor had the biologist teaching the class. In fact, no one did back then. I put the first one we caught at Salleyland in a plastic sandwich bag filled with swamp water to take to the cabin to check a field guide to confirm that I had identified it correctly and to find out more about its biology. A plastic bag filled with water is an excellent way to keep a fish alive as well as observe it and show it to others.

Fish biologists have speculated on the function of this odd placement of the vent in pirate perches since it was first described in 1824. Two centuries later scientists from SREL published their findings from a study of the pirate perch in its murky habitat. They used modern technology, including underwater filming and DNA analysis in the laboratory, to identify the parents of various offspring. Their discoveries were made in the cool waters of late winter and early spring when pirate perches begin spawning in the Southeast.

The study revealed why a fish would have a vent located in the front of the body instead of toward the back. They documented for the first time that the female thrusts her head into a tangled root mass and lays her eggs, a behavior unconfirmed for any other North American fish. The male quickly follows suit, putting his head into the same opening in the roots and depositing sperm to fertilize the eggs. We will likely never know the evolutionary pathways that led to a fish sticking its head into a root mass to lay and fertilize eggs and having a vent that accommodates the process. However, *why* the opening through which a pirate perch deposits eggs or sperm moves forward has been adequately explained.

The story of how a combination of ecology, technology, and genetics explained the peculiar placement of the vent provides plenty to tell visitors about a pirate perch when we catch one. But these little fish have another trait that adds to their mystique. Pirate perches trick their prey—water beetles, mosquito larvae, and other swamp denizens—in a manner never before described for a fish: chemical camouflage. Countless animals, both predators and prey, use visual camouflage to make themselves hard to detect by other animals. But vision is not the only sense animals use to identify enemies or locate prey. Some tropical bats eat frogs, homing in on them at night when they are calling. In response, some frogs have become ventriloquists, making it difficult for a bat to use its echolocation abilities to pinpoint their would-be prey's location. The frogs are using auditory camouflage.

Two ecologists, William J. Resetarits Jr. (University of Mississippi) and Christopher A. Binckley (Arcadia University), conducted an innovative study that revealed an unexpected trait of pirate perches. In the carefully designed experiment, treefrogs were given the choice of laying their eggs in a wading pool containing fish or in a pool devoid of fish smells. Many fish will eat frog eggs and tadpoles, so the smell of fish is a signal to frogs that the site is not a favorable one. The frogs in the study chose to lay eggs in the pools with no fish. The exception was that if only a pirate perch was in the pool, the frogs laid their eggs anyway. Whatever chemical cues most fish emit, which the treefrogs could detect, were camouflaged.

The investigators also conducted studies with two kinds of common water beetles with similar results. Both avoided pools with the chemical smell of fish. Not so when only pirate perches lurked in the pool. The beetles were unable to detect their presence, even though the little fish would readily eat them. Certain insects use chemical camouflage strategies by emitting smells targeted toward another specific insect to whom they do not want to reveal their presence. But the pirate perch has a generalized approach, in essence having an invisibility cloak, so none of its numerous prey can detect it.

Pirate perches are fascinating creatures in many ways. Having nonvisual camouflage as part of their arsenal for deceiving prey adds to their mystique. Research scientists who unlock nature's mysteries have revealed why the fish's vent moves up the body and demonstrated its ability to make itself undetectable. Anyone showing an audience a pirate perch in a plastic bag has plenty to talk about.

Welcome All Visitors

Anne Gibbons, Bill Fitts, and I checked the trashcan traps I set out last night. A coiled cottonmouth on the bridge sidled into the water, and another was in the trap looking up expectantly, waiting for its close-up. We took photos of it and a bunch of crawfish also in the trap. Lots of dragonflies and damselflies patrolled the edges of the stream, and an Acadian flycatcher flitted around us. We photographed a mating pair of phantom crane flies and were greeted by a blue-tailed five-lined skink when we got back to the porch, before eating the paninis we had brought.

SALLEYLAND FIELD NOTES, JUNE 17, 2017

SPECIAL TIMES ARISE WHEN PREMEDITATED SOLITUDE IS THE ORDER OF the day. Communing with oneself while drifting down a stream, walking in winter woods, or watching busy pollinators on autumn goldenrods in a sandy field can revitalize one's spirit. On the other hand, discovering a red-bellied snake under a coverboard, locating russula mushrooms in damp woods, or finding golden-club flowers at the edge of a stream is more enjoyable with a companion or two.

Finding an unusual species, observing odd behavior, or musing about nature's mysteries is more fulfilling if someone experiences it with you. In my case, I often leave the scene by knowing more about what we have encountered because of someone else's knowledge, a natural history question I had never considered, or a deeper ecological thinking about what we have observed. Having company enriches a wildlife field trip. Sometimes it helps to have someone along to back up an improbable sounding adventure or discovery.

I have invited many friends, colleagues, classes, and organizations to

Salleyland, and I am pleased when they consider their time on the land well spent. I particularly enjoy introducing visitors to the first yellow-billed cuckoo (also known as a rain crow) they have ever heard, the first bluespotted sunfish they have ever seen, or the first eastern musk turtle (also known as a stinkpot) they have ever smelled. Tasting a green persimmon is certain to leave them with a lingering and vivid memory.

Having a companion enjoy nature's offerings with you often leads to the most satisfying experiences. If you have a place that lends itself to inviting others to join you in the wild, do so.

Invite Nature Societies

Groups of people focused on a particular taxonomic group, habitat, or specific locale across the country number in the thousands. Many are formal organizations, often with the word Friends, Association, or Society as part of the name. The members of some are primarily professional whereas others are composed of amateurs. Organizations can be found at the state, regional, and national level. Some but not all require dues. New groups are created every week, month, and year as like-minded citizens find each other and recognize their common interest in some unifying aspect of natural history. Group size varies from a few participants to thousands. Nearly all started with one or two people who felt a calling.

Members of SCAN (South Carolina Association of Naturalists) left a significant mark on Salleyland, not because of what they took but because of what they left—their collective knowledge of the wildlife surrounding us day and night. In discussions with some of the members prior to the weekend field trip, I learned that I would be able to add significantly to my inventory of an important group of insects during the visit—beetles. Finding beetles does not require much expertise, which is not surprising when considering the little hard-shelled creatures have more described species than any other animal group in the world—350,000! More than 30,000 are known from the United States. That we were able to find a few at Salleyland came as no surprise. They ranged in size from tiny orange flea beetles that eat aquatic vegetation to a large mahogany-colored stag beetle with pincers, which the males use in combat with each other.

We were fortunate to have beetle expert Jan Ciegler with us not only to show us techniques for finding beetles but also to identify those we found.

The so-called stinky can traps she set out to attract carrion beetles at night were the most memorable to me—an alcohol-filled can of decomposing flesh. No one was willing to get close enough to ID the bait. Whatever the rotting meat was it definitely lured a variety of carrion beetles.

Some were large red-and-black burying beetles, which bury dead mice and birds underground, out of sight of other animals that might make a meal of the corpse. The beetles then lay eggs around the entombed carcass, which their larvae feast on during their development. Jan also found a few hister beetles that were attracted to the putrid cans. These black beetles are one of the insects used in entomological forensics to determine how long a body has been dead. I'm not sure what the total number of beetles will be when all identifications are complete, but upon preliminary examination we have scores maybe even hundreds of species at Salleyland.

SCAN members who were experts in other taxonomic groups offered further insights into the biodiversity of Salleyland. I was shown my first blazing star aster flower, with its eye-catching reddish-purple flowers. The versatile plant has been described as attractive whether cut or dried. I was pleased to see them living. A pipevine swallowtail made an appearance one day. Two SCAN members with lepidopteran leanings pointed out the difference between it and other black-winged swallowtails in the region. I appreciated the interconnectedness of the plant and animal worlds when I realized a favored food of pipevine caterpillars is Virginia snakeroot, a plant someone had discovered earlier at Salleyland.

Many visitors were there for the herpetological opportunities, having heard of the abundance and high species diversity of reptiles and amphibians. That weekend we found twenty-three, including ten species of snakes, which is a respectable diversity anywhere. No matter what group of organisms you are most passionate about, engage with some kind of wildlife group that goes out into the real world. If you cannot invite them on a field trip, join them on theirs. Nature groups across the country and around the world generally welcome new members and enjoy interacting with people who have an interest in wild things. With luck, you will learn from each other.

Seek out a natural history group looking for an opportunity to go somewhere their animals, plants, or mushrooms of interest can be found. The flip side is to find an organization that sparks your interest and gathers for field trips. Either way, if they can't come to you, go to them.

The Salamander Club Is Getting Started

I received an email inviting me to join the Salamander Club. I was honored, though the invitation did not come from a prestigious international society of amphibian scientists. It was sent by a seven-year-old named Logan. I felt especially privileged because I would be only the third member of the club. The other member was Logan's twin brother, Blake.

We planned the inaugural meeting of the club for November, a good time for finding salamanders. Before we began our trip to where I thought the best habitat would be to seek out our quarry, Logan showed me his salamander scrapbook. He had internet photos of newts, tiger salamanders, and many others. The book also contained a handwritten, second-grade block print copy of the Salamander Pledge: "I promise to take care of salamanders at all times." I agreed to honor the pledge, as I hope anyone would do.

We spent a few minutes looking at the scrapbook and discussing some of the finer points about salamanders, one of two major groups of US amphibians, the other being the frogs and toads. We talked about how big salamanders can get. The scrapbook had a photo of one of the largest in the world, the Japanese giant salamander, which can reach a length of nearly five feet. We considered what our local salamanders might eat—earthworms, bugs, smaller salamanders. And, of course, the most important question for the day—how do you catch a salamander? This turned out to be a central issue. Two-thirds of the club had never seen a salamander in the wild.

I suggested we go into the swamp to a place where I thought we might remedy that situation. I brought along eleven-year-old Nick, who agreed to lead the way to a place where we might have some success. We set out over the wooden bridge leading into the swamp from our cabin. Any concerns I had about the twins hesitating to venture into a swamp a day after several inches of rain had fallen soon vanished. They were real troopers. They followed close behind Nick, and I heard not one complaint about wet feet when they stepped into deep holes and swamp water poured into their boots.

We eventually reached higher ground where Nick and I had previously put out coverboards. Coverboards, in this case squares of plywood, are one way to find certain kinds of salamanders. Reptiles, amphibians, and many other animals seek refuge under them. Nick picked out a board and turned it over. Success! Beneath the board were two salamanders. One was a yellow one with black stripes (a three-lined salamander); the other was bright red with yellow eyes (an eastern red salamander). Each of the twins picked up one of the salamanders after receiving instructions on how to do so. The awe in their eyes was marvelous. We put the salamanders in plastic bags to which Nick had added sphagnum moss and took them back to the cabin for a closer look.

I do not know if this will be the first step on a career path for either boy, but their early display of a conservation ethic and their fascination with the natural world are impressive. The twins' experience sends an environmental message to parents of young children. They would not have such enthusiasm for looking at animals in their natural habitats were it not for parental encouragement. The boys did not whine or complain when they got wet and dirty in our trek through the swamp. Kudos to their parents.

Nick and I ended our field trip with the boys by explaining to them the importance of returning an animal to its home if possible after capturing it. Following that advice, Nick retrieved the plastic bags with the two salamanders and returned them to their swamp coverboard. When he returned from his solo trip through the swamp, the twins invited him to become a member of the Salamander Club. Teaching them how to find and identify the first salamanders of their herpetological careers probably earned him his invitation. Taking the pledge assured him a position as salamander guide for the next trip.

Invite Teachers and Students

Mike was on the tin roof of the cabin cleaning the fall and winter leaves out of the gutter when Joe Pechmann and his herpetology class from Western Carolina University arrived in three big white vans. As the students emerged from the vehicles and eased onto the deck, Mike stood up and waved at Joe before reaching down to clear the final few feet of gutter. He picked up the last handful of soggy oak and hickory leaves, exclaimed in surprise, then held up a three-foot rat snake that had been nestled in the debris. Joe and the students did their own exclaiming. Some may have thought Mike had staged the capture for their arrival. Not so. He was as surprised as the rest of us. Great start for a bunch of college students who had come to Salleyland to find as many herps as they could in a day. The rat snake constricting around Mike's arm was the first on the list.

Joe is one of several college professors we have invited to use Salleyland for class field trips in herpetology, vertebrate ecology, and other wildlife biology courses. When the trip is in April, it is almost certain to introduce students to numerous plants and animals, many or most of which they have never seen before, including species as common as rat snakes.

Field trips to explore the outdoors offer valuable connections to the natural environment. Many biology majors these days are unaccustomed to being outdoors and experiencing wildlife firsthand. A large proportion are from urban or suburban areas and had limited opportunities to spend time in wild areas as children. Based on my twenty years of annual talks to the forty incoming biology honors students at the University of Georgia, more than 98 percent of them had never seen a live salamander in the wild. I determined that the majority were from suburbs in the greater Atlanta area or comparable urban settings elsewhere.

Another reason many college students, including those in graduate programs in biology, do not acquire field experience is that the academic institution itself de-emphasizes the importance of natural history. Many universities now follow a business model and are more supportive of biology departments that emphasize research in molecular biology and genetics because funding opportunities in these fields far exceed those of grants given for environmental studies. Disturbingly, many colleges have become so excessively litigation conscious that some professors are reluctant to risk an overnight trip bearing responsibility for a bunch of kids in their late teens or early twenties. I applaud all teachers who take their chances in giving students real-life experiences of the natural world.

Joe has brought his herpetology class to Salleyland for many years. Parker was invited to tag along with the class the first year. Following his performance on that field trip Joe has checked on Parker's availability before scheduling the class visit. During each year's herpetology class field trip, Joe puts forth a challenge suggested by one of his students. I recommend the approach to anyone teaching a field course. At the end of the trip, the class votes on which student made the most outstanding herpetofaunal discovery or capture of the day or otherwise proved themselves by being an exemplary field biologist. The winner receives a herpetological field guide.

The first year at Salleyland the class comprised a mix of graduate and undergraduate students. Parker qualified as a student because he was in the eighth grade. During the day he proved himself to be an extraordinary field biologist. He found and showed the class of eighteen students what was, for most of them, the first Chamberlain's dwarf salamander, mud salamander, glass lizard, and cottonmouth they had ever seen in the wild. He cinched the outstanding capture award when he encouraged Daniel Sollenberger, a recent graduate who had returned for the field trip, to wade across the creek with him through waist-deep muck and vegetation. A couple of college students followed.

When the four reached the point at which the floating mat of aquatic plants margined the stream, they prepared to start swimming the last fifty feet or so across the stream. Those of us taking the dry land route watched from the highway bridge as Parker abruptly lunged forward. After plenty of splashing and thrashing, he emerged with a large brown watersnake clutched midbody. Brown watersnakes are a native species noted for catching catfish as a major part of their diet. Although the snakes are common in some rivers and streams in a few southeastern states, most of the class had never seen one. As Daniel moved forward to make sure Parker had not mistakenly grabbed a cottonmouth, Parker dove away from him into the creek and grabbed another large snake that was drifting by. Shoulder deep in the stream, Parker held his two captives above his head like a referee signaling a touchdown. Daniel relaxed as he saw it also was not a cottonmouth but a southern banded watersnake. I had not been particularly concerned. I knew Parker could tell the difference between the various look-alike species. Daniel nominated Parker for the field trip prize and the class vote was unanimous.

Teachers from Davidson College, South Carolina State, University of Georgia, Duke University, and others have led field courses at Salleyland. We have invited numerous students participating in courses or conducting ecological field research to visit. Many have made such requests on their own, requests that are always welcome. If you have access to natural field sites where teachers can bring their students, invite them for a visit. A bunch of students loosed into a field setting and surrounded by a diversity of plants and animals can lead to a contagious enthusiasm that is good for them and you. If you decide to offer a field guide to the best participant, that's a good idea, too.

It's Only a Tree

Some visitors to Salleyland have contributed to environmental awareness and appreciation in unexpected ways. One of the more unanticipated occurred when a country music singer sat with Parker and me on the porch overlooking the creek.

Okefenokee Joe "left the city a long time ago" for reasons he "need not disclose." For ten years he made his home in the Okefenokee Swamp, living his dream "the way a man oughta, happy with each day that goes by." He is also a marvelous singer and storyteller. His best-selling song is "Swampwise." He is a naturalist, an ardent environmentalist, and very definitely swampwise.

Okefenokee Joe's real name is Dick Flood, a noted singer and song-writer who left the Nashville music scene many years ago and took up residence on the Georgia side of the Okefenokee Swamp. He lived in the wilds with the plants and animals and learned what they had to tell him. He now has a house in the woods near Salleyland, about a mile or so from the cabin, and we have enjoyed having an occasional cup of coffee together.

In one of his albums, Joe focuses on his appreciation for nature and the interconnectedness of animals, plants, and the natural ecosystems they all depend on. One of my favorites is "It's Only a Tree." I like it not only because it is a melodious tune sung by a fine artist but also because it has an important environmental message.

The opening lines remind us that the natural world is linked together in ways that may not be obvious to humans—something we should all strive to remember.

> It's only a tree just one more tree,
> Who cares if it lives or it dies?
> It's only a tree, what's one less tree
> Who'd miss it? You'd be surprised.

Joe proceeds to answer the question of who would miss the tree by pointing out how one species' dependency leads to the secondary dependency of another. White-tailed deer eat the leaves of purple flowers that grow in the tree's shade, and Joe notes that if we "take away the tree, the flower grows no more / The deer must find another place to graze."

Parker, who knows many of Joe's songs, was at the cabin one day when Joe was visiting. They sang "Swampy the Dog" together, and then we talked awhile about deer and trees and streams and snakes. Joe caught a lot of snakes when he lived in the Okefenokee Swamp and gave educational presentations to schools and nature groups. Joe was hobbling a bit on that particular visit but wanted to see a snake. He asked Parker if he could catch one and bring it to where we were sitting. I wanted a photograph of the two of them holding one. Parker went out in the canoe, paddling beneath the overhanging vegetation, confident he would find something. He soon returned with a rough green snake he found on a tree limb overhanging the stream.

"Its branches reach out to all those in need. / A spider spins its web." Green snakes are climbers and eat spiders. Interconnectedness.

When I think about the connections that create food webs throughout ecosystems, I recall other lines from Joe's tree song. "The otter eats the fish that ate the dancing fly / Born in the cocoon up in that tree." We have otters and fish in our creek, and plenty of insects. The complexity of energy flow within natural ecosystems is remarkable—one species depends on another, which depends on another, and so on. We need to keep these natural systems intact and contaminant-free.

Some animals and plants are so rare or lead such clandestine lives that we may only experience them once in a lifetime, if that. Others are always present. Still others come and go with the seasons, reappearing on a regular basis. Animals in each category depend on trees for nesting or safety or food. The ebony jewelwing damselflies flit in the shade of trees in the swamp; bright yellow prothonotary warblers nest in tree holes along streams; and mistletoe, sporting berries that cedar waxwings eat, grows on trees big and small. We are fortunate to have all of those along our tree-lined stream. Wherever you are, take a look at a tree and consider how its web of life has many pathways, many branches.

The South Carolina Herpetological Society (now South Carolina Partners in Amphibian and Reptile Conservation) conducted a weekend bioblitz at Salleyland that yielded thirty-five species of reptiles and amphibians. Photo by Mike Gibbons.

Okefenokee Joe uses his songs and stories to help spread his environmental message, a message that ought to be heeded by anyone who appreciates the intricacies of nature—which should be all of us. "Life is intertwined, and somewhere down the line / Somehow we're all connected to that tree." The significance is easy to see when you walk in the woods or alongside a stream.

Do a Bioblitz

Any wildlife enthusiast interested in getting new records of what species inhabit a piece of property should conduct a bioblitz. The model is simple and straightforward—invite a group of naturalist friends or an organization with a taxonomically eclectic membership to come for whatever period of time you agree upon. Turn them loose to verify the presence of any wildlife they can find. Arm them with lists of species known to be present at the site and those potentially present but not yet discovered.

I decided a Salleyland bioblitz focused on reptiles and amphibians would be a welcome exercise. It would document the presence of some species and possibly discover new ones. Whatever the case, a bioblitz has two positive features. One is to inform the property owner of a baseline of presence, distribution, and abundance of selected taxonomic groups. The other is to provide individuals an admirable mission for a field trip. Arranging a herp bioblitz was not difficult. I invited Tess Moody, president of the South Carolina Herpetological Society (SCHS; now South Carolina Partners in Amphibian and Reptile Conservation), to organize a weekend event. Conducting bioblitzes at different times of the year can provide comparisons of seasonal activity. For the first one, we selected May, always a good month for herping. An easy next step was to decide on a size limit for how many could attend—twenty-five. A larger crowd can be difficult to manage, and it limits the experience each individual has with the species you encounter.

I watched the array of tents, campers, and hammocks go up in the area around the cabin. Clearly these people had done this before. Tess provided each participant with a list of ethics and safety guidelines, an important consideration for anyone having a group of individuals descend on a wildlife habitat (see appendix 3). The visitors had varying levels of experience; all were focused on finding as many reptiles and amphibians as they could. And they did. Anyone who found a frog, salamander, lizard, turtle, or nonvenomous snake was encouraged to bring it to the cabin so others could take photographs. Although several in the group were trained in handling them, venomous snakes were to be observed in place. Each animal was later released at the spot where it was captured. We found a total of thirty-five reptile and amphibian species during the field trip, a respectably high species diversity of herpetofauna to be found in one weekend anywhere in the United States. Most of the group got to see the six cottonmouths in the swamp and an enormous canebrake rattlesnake hiding under a piece of tin. The total of all captures was more than a hundred, including twenty-nine snakes, a prize for most field herpetologists.

The list of new species of Salleyland herps, which had been accumulated over several years, did not increase during the herp bioblitz. But the second capture of a special amphibian (two-toed amphiuma) was documented, confirming the presence of this remarkable creature in the swamp. Having grown up in Alabama and being interested in herpetology from a young age, I learned early about amphiumas, giant salamanders (the largest ones are more than three feet long) that inhabit the swamps and lowlands of the Southeast. If you look in a field guide, it will be referred to as an amphiuma, because like so many animals and plants that are unfamiliar to most people, the scientific name becomes the so-called common name. Even most herpetologists in the country have never seen an amphiuma in the wild, yet these unusual amphibians with four tiny legs the size of toothpicks have an important role in food webs wherever they occur—they are the preferred prey of mud snakes. During the SCHS herp bioblitz, Parker jumped off the bridge into the creek one night and grabbed a mud snake to show the group. We knew amphiumas had to be out there somewhere.

On any field trip, even one targeting a particular taxonomic group, you should pay attention to all wildlife discoveries, and some SCHS members had extensive experience with other organisms. Jake Zadik added a new insect for the land, a Cyrano darner, a blue-eyed dragonfly. Juliana Smith added several moths to the Salleyland lists and a bird, a yellow-breasted chat, once accepted as North America's largest warbler. Recent research has created phylogenetic uncertainty about the species. The chat is no longer considered a warbler. It is thought be more closely related to New World blackbirds. Perhaps the most remarkable creatures encountered that weekend were two creepy horsehair worms. Tess and Parker each found one at the edge of the stream one night.

Horsehair worms belong to a poorly understood group of organisms with more than three hundred species. They are in their own separate phylum and their biological relationship to other worms is ambiguous. The ones Parker and Tess caught were adults, each the diameter of a piano wire and about two feet long in a twisted knotty mess. Horsehair worms are special because they are so unspecialized. They have no digestive system, no respiratory system, and no circulatory system. They are free-living, meaning they are not parasitic. But the larvae are.

In some species, and probably in those we had, the adults mate and reproduce in water where the female lays eggs that float. If an egg is eaten by an insect and then hatches, the tiny parasitic larva drills its way out of the insect's intestine and takes up residence in the body cavity. It feeds on the inside of the insect until it grows into a long worm ready to start the cycle again. Imagine a two-foot-long worm inside a grasshopper! Even more bizarre: how does the worm know it will end up in water so it can mate? A study on hairworms that infect crickets and grasshoppers offers a partial explanation.

In laboratory studies the investigators found that the hairworm parasite actually alters the behavior of the insect by producing molecules that enter the insect's central nervous system. The exact mechanisms are unknown, but chemical alterations in the brain make the insect jump into water and drown. Such abnormal insect behavior puts the now-developed worm where it wants to be, back in the water where the adults emerge from their host. Brainwashing at its most effective. Fortunately, hairworm parasites have little use for people, although rare infections have been reported in medical and parasitological scientific journals.

Our herp bioblitz was an outstanding success. People engaged fully in the process of finding as many reptiles and amphibians as possible. No one was disappointed. A bonus came through experiences with wildlife in addition to herpetofauna. Every field trip should be approached with the idea of achieving a goal—with the understanding that no serendipitous encounters will go uninvestigated.

What Have We Learned
and How Does It End?

WILDLIFE ADVENTURES IN NATURAL HABITATS WILL BE A CONTINUING saga at Salleyland. The land has already provided many lessons and will continue to do so. Fascinating ecological experiences beckon wherever we are. Nature shows on TV often extol the bizarre, but you need not be in Australia, Africa, or under the sea to witness extraordinary and exciting wildlife encounters. Ecological mysteries can present themselves on any piece of land, any body of water, anywhere in the world, even in a temperate zone habitat rather than the biologically diverse tropics. Simple rural

Nick (*left*) and Parker examine frog eggs found in a wet area alongside the creek. Children have an innate curiosity about the natural world that should be encouraged whenever and wherever possible. Photo by author.

settings and suburban neighborhoods offer their own opportunities for nature walks. Curious children, amateur naturalists, and credentialed professionals alike can enjoy exploring the outdoors.

Running through this book from beginning (I celebrate the joy so many of us feel when we are outdoors) to end (communing with oneself while drifting down a stream . . . can revitalize one's spirit) is a sense of the restorative power of the natural world. Books, essays, and research studies extol nature's curative and uplifting potential to anyone paying her a visit. John Byrd's essay "On Being Outside" (www.cresosnake.com/on-being-outside) offers a concise summary of how being outside can enhance one's overall physical, mental, and emotional well-being. Possible benefits of being in natural settings, supported by a variety of reputable sources, include lowering blood pressure and reducing stress, improving "the attention of kids with ADHD," boosting short-term memory, and promoting positive moods. I have observed all of these phenomena in visitors to the land.

Salleyland has schooled many of us in the ways of nature, reminding us that we should be prepared for the unexpected at any time. As our version of the saying goes, "Always remember to never say never or always about wildlife and animal behavior." Rules do exist. But rules have exceptions. Even the exceptions have exceptions. One reason the rules of biology and subsequently ecology become so convoluted is that humans thrive on order and consistency, but animals and plants do not always follow the rules. And they give us no explanation for why they don't do so. Life on Earth today is the product of more than a billion years of evolution, with many twists and turns along the way. Natural selection, through survival of the fittest coupled with chance, has resulted in myriad strategies for species to survive under both predictable and unpredictable circumstances. Many paths have been taken to get where any species is today. That includes humans. Some of those paths may lead to stochastic dead ends. That doesn't mean we can't encounter them in the wild and wonder at what we have found. Do not be discouraged if you can't identify some plant or don't know why an animal is behaving in a certain way. You needn't have all the answers to enjoy what nature has to offer.

Making lists can be a pleasurable, lifelong exercise. I encourage everyone who enjoys the outdoors and its array of life-forms to keep records of what you find. Pick taxonomic groups of special interest and focus on them while appreciating the bycatch. I will keep looking for reptile and amphibian species at Salleyland in hopes of increasing our list beyond the fifty-six species we reached in 2020 (see appendix 1). At least a dozen species of herpetofauna indigenous to the southeastern region where Salleyland sits are absent from our records. For example, the seldom-seen rainbow snake with its stunning coloration is likely to show up one day, or night. I have caught them within thirty miles of Salleyland in creeks similar to ours. We have caught American eels, the primary prey of adult rainbow snakes, in our creek. The snakes will not go hungry. The subliminal thought that any coverboard turned over in the swamp might yield a rainbow snake will keep herpetologists, as well as botanists and mushroom collectors, turning over the next one. I'm counting on adding a rainbow snake to our herp list at Salleyland.

People are far from unraveling all of nature's mysteries. Exciting new discoveries will continue to be made, day and night, season to season. Not just at Salleyland but everywhere in the natural world. My original goal, to

Students in a University of Georgia wildlife techniques class learn how to set hoop traps in the creek for turtles. Traps are baited with punctured sardine cans. An empty bottle is placed in each trap to keep one end afloat so turtles can breathe should the trap collapse while set. Photo by author.

find herpetofauna, soon gave way to a broader objective: to embrace the natural history of all wildlife.

A collateral benefit of beginning the Salleyland herp inventory was watching youngsters develop an interest in wildlife biology in general, not just the target species. You do not always find a reptile or amphibian, but nature is full of other treasures. I watched Nick marvel at a dinner-plate-size bolete, the largest mushroom either of us had ever seen. Sam was delighted with the beauty of a bluespotted sunfish he caught in a dip net. Parker's discovery of a bald-faced hornet's nest turned a non-herp day into a successful outing. Allison's delight when she caught her first male fence lizard and saw its brilliant blue belly confirmed why reptiles and amphibians remain at the forefront of our favorite species. As the grandkids' enthusiasm for all elements of natural habitats grew, I observed a ripple effect. They encouraged friends and their friends' parents to come on field trips, adding to the support base for wildlife conservation and increasing our odds of new finds at Salleyland. Try to include children in your wildlife excursions. You will be well rewarded.

Parker (*left*), Sam, and Nick fish from the Salleyland
bridge (2021). Photo by Mike Gibbons.

A word about the process of getting children involved. I began by teaching the grandchildren about the animals themselves, introducing them to a diversity of species when I had live ones on hand. My objective was not to teach the children to identify every species but to instill a sense of wonder about them all, especially reptiles and amphibians. Once I began taking them on field trips to Salleyland or local parks or the backyard, finding the animals was easy.

They quickly and enthusiastically learned how to turn over coverboards, use dip nets, check aquatic traps, open bird boxes, and simply walk around to see what there was to see. They soon began to catch and hold animals so they could be identified. Potential environmental hazards are part of the fabric of wildlife biology. Adults as well as children should view such hazards not with trepidation but with practical knowledge of how to avoid them. My helpers' understanding and ready acceptance of basic safety instructions—such as, do not handle or even get near a venomous snake—was reassuring. Learning not to step in fire ant nests or wear short pants when walking through stinging nettle requires only one self-taught lesson.

Follow your taxonomic passion. And while doing so learn to appreciate all wildlife you encounter. One overriding benefit of my wildlife experiences at Salleyland is that they have kept a retired herpetologist happily occupied and promise to do so for the foreseeable future.

Reptiles and Amphibians
at Salleyland

FOLLOWING ARE COMMON AND SCIENTIFIC NAMES OF 56 REPTILES AND amphibians found during a herpetofaunal inventory at Salleyland.*

AMPHIBIANS (20 SPECIES)
  Frogs and Toads (10)
    family Bufonidae (toads)
      southern toad (*Anaxyrus* [a.k.a. *Bufo*] *terrestris*)
    family Hylidae (treefrogs)
      Cope's gray treefrog (*Hyla* [a.k.a. *Dryophytes*] *chrysoscelis*)
      green treefrog (*Hyla* [a.k.a. *Dryophytes*] *cinerea*)
      southern cricket frog (*Acris gryllus*)
      spring peeper (*Pseudacris crucifer*)
      squirrel treefrog (*Hyla* [a.k.a. *Dryophytes*] *squirella*)
    family Microhylidae (narrowmouth toads)
      eastern narrowmouth toad (*Gastrophryne carolinensis*)
    family Ranidae (true frogs)
      bullfrog (*Rana* [a.k.a. *Lithobates*] *catesbeiana*)
      green/bronze frog (*Rana* [a.k.a. *Lithobates*] *clamitans*)
      southern leopard frog (*Rana* [a.k.a. *Lithobates*] *sphenocephala*)
  Salamanders (10)
    family Amphiumidae (amphiumas)

---

*Note: Animals have not changed their morphology, ecology, or behavior for millennia. Humans, however, have been changing the names of animals, as well as plants, every year for over two centuries. Genetic research has allowed scientists to discover new species and to recognize changes in perceived phylogenetic relationships within some genera and families. Taxonomy is in a state of flux. Name changes recommended by one authority are not always well received by others. The names given in appendix 1 and appendix 2 were accepted by most authoritative sources at the time of publication and will lead readers to information about the animal, plant, or mushroom, no matter what people want to call it.

two-toed amphiuma (*Amphiuma means*)
family Plethodontidae (lungless salamanders)
    Chamberlain's dwarf salamander (*Eurycea chamberlaini*)
    many-lined salamander (*Stereochilus marginatus*)
    mud salamander (*Pseudotriton montanus*)
    red salamander (*Pseudotriton ruber*)
    slimy salamander (*Plethodon glutinosus* complex; *P. chlorobryonis*)
    southern two-lined salamander (*Eurycea cirrigera*)
    three-lined salamander (*Eurycea guttolineata*)
family Sirenidae (sirens)
    greater siren (*Siren lacertina*)
    lesser siren (*Siren intermedia*)

Reptiles (36 species)

Lizards (8)

family Anguidae (legless and alligator lizards)
    eastern glass lizard (*Ophisaurus ventralis*)
family Dactyloidae (anoles)
    green anole (*Anolis carolinensis*)
family Phrynosomatidae (spiny and horned lizards)
    eastern fence lizard (*Sceloporus undulatus*)
family Scincidae (skinks)
    broad-headed skink (*Plestiodon* [a.k.a. *Eumeces*] *laticeps*)
    five-lined skink (*Plestiodon* [a.k.a. *Eumeces*] *fasciatus*)
    ground (little brown) skink (*Scincella lateralis*)
    southeastern five-lined skink (*Plestiodon* [a.k.a. *Eumeces*]
      inexpectatus)
family Teiidae (racerunners)
    six-lined racerunner (*Aspidoscelis* [a.k.a. *Cnemidophorus*]
      sexlineatus)

Snakes (22)

family Colubridae (nonvenomous snakes)
    banded watersnake (*Nerodia fasciata*)
    black racer (*Coluber constrictor*)
    brown snake (*Storeria dekayi*)
    brown watersnake (*Nerodia taxispilota*)
    corn snake (*Pantherophis* [a.k.a. *Elaphe*] *guttatus*)
    eastern coachwhip (*Masticophis* [a.k.a. *Coluber*] *flagellum*)

eastern garter snake (*Thamnophis sirtalis*)
eastern hognose snake (*Heterodon platirhinos*)
eastern kingsnake (*Lampropeltis getula*)
mud snake (*Farancia abacura*)
pine snake (*Pituophis melanoleucus*)
queen snake (*Regina septemvittata*)
rat snake (*Pantherophis* [a.k.a. *Elaphe*] *obsoletus*)
red-bellied snake (*Storeria occipitomaculata*)
red-bellied watersnake (*Nerodia erythrogaster*)
ringneck snake (*Diadophis punctatus*)
rough green snake (*Opheodrys aestivus*)
scarlet snake (*Cemophora coccinea*)
southeastern crowned snake (*Tantilla coronata*)
family Viperidae (vipers)
canebrake/timber rattlesnake (*Crotalus horridus*)
copperhead (*Agkistrodon contortrix*)
cottonmouth/water moccasin (*Agkistrodon piscivorus*)

Turtles (6)
family Chelydridae (snapping turtles)
common snapping turtle (*Chelydra serpentina*)
family Emydidae (basking turtles)
box turtle (*Terrapene carolina*)
slider turtle (*Trachemys scripta*)
family Kinosternidae (mud and musk turtles)
common musk turtle (*Sternotherus odoratus*)
eastern mud turtle (*Kinosternon subrubrum*)
striped mud turtle (*Kinosternon baurii*)

Plants, Animals, and Mushrooms at Salleyland

F OLLOWING ARE COMMON AND SCIENTIFIC NAMES OF PLANTS, ANIMALS other than reptiles and amphibians, and mushrooms at Salleyland that are mentioned in this book.*

Acadian flycatcher (*Empidonax virescens*)
American bur-reed (*Sparganium americanum*)
American crow (*Corvus brachyrhynchos*)
American holly (*Ilex opaca*)
American snowbell (*Styrax americana*)
armadillo, nine-banded (*Dasypus novemcinctus*)
attenuated bluet (*Enallagma daeckii*)
bald cypress (*Taxodium distichum*)
bald eagle (*Haliaeetus leucocephalus*)
bald-faced hornet (*Dolichovespula maculata*)
barred owl (*Strix varia*)
basilica orb weaver (*Mecynogea lemniscata*)
beautyberry (*Callicarpa americana*)
beaver (*Castor canadensis*)
blackberry (*Rubus* sp.)
black cherry (*Prunus serotina*)
blazing star (*Liatris spicata*)
blue ghost (*Phausis reticulata*)
blue jay (*Cyanocitta cristata*)
bluespotted sunfish (*Enneacanthus gloriosus*)
bobcat (*Lynx rufus*)
broadleaf arrowhead (*Sagittaria latifolia*)

*See the appendix 1 footnote concerning plant, animal, and mushroom names.

brook silverside (*Labidesthes sicculus*)
brown-and-yellow millipede (*Apheloria* sp.)
burying beetle (*Nicrophorus tomentosus* and *N. orbicollis*)
caddisfly (order Trichoptera)
Carolina cherry laurel (*Prunus caroliniana*)
Carolina chickadee (*Poecile carolinensis*)
Carolina jasmine (*Gelsemium sempervirens*)
Carolina wild pink (*Silene caroliniana*)
Carolina wren (*Thryothorus ludovicianus*)
cattail (*Typha latifolia*)
cedar waxwing (*Bombycilla cedrorum*)
cherry millipede (*Sigmoria* sp.)
chironomid fly larva (order Diptera)
cinnamon fern (*Osmundastrum cinnamomeum*)
cloudless sulfur butterfly (*Phoebis sennae*)
common whitetail (*Plathemis lydia*)
crabapple (*Malus* sp.)
crane fly (family Tipulidae)
crawfish (family Cambaridae)
Cyrano darner (*Nasiaeschna pentacantha*)
deer, white-tailed (*Odocoileus virginianus*)
doghobble (*Leucothoe axillaris*)
dogwood, flowering (*Cornus florida*)
duck potato (*Sagittaria latifolia*)
duckweed firetail (*Telebasis byersi*)
eastern bluebird (*Sialia sialis*)
eastern mud minnow (*Umbra pygmaea*)
eastern pondhawk (*Erythemis simplicicollis*)
eastern red bat (*Lasiurus borealis*)
eastern red cedar (*Juniperus virginiana*)
eastern woodrat (*Neotoma floridana*)
ebony jewelwing (*Calopteryx maculata*)
evening bat (*Nycticeius humeralis*)
false turkey tail mushroom (*Stereum ostrea*)
fingernail clam (family Sphaeridae)
fishing spider (*Dolomedes* sp.)
flowering dogwood (*Cornus florida*)
fox squirrel (*Sciurus niger*)

freshwater grass shrimp (*Palaemonetes paludosus*)
freshwater mussel (*Elliptio complanata* and *E. icterina*)
funnel web spider (family Agelenidae)
giant leopard moth (*Hypercompe scribonia*)
goldenrod (*Solidago* sp.)
golden silk orb weaver (*Nephila* sp.)
gray fox (*Urocyon cinereoargenteus*)
gray squirrel (*Sciurus carolinensis*)
great crested flycatcher (*Myiarchus crinitus*)
green arrow arum (*Peltandra virginica*)
greenbrier (*Smilax* sp.)
greenstriped mapleworm (*Dryocampa rubicunda*)
hackberry (*Celtis laevigata*)
hister beetle (*Euspilotus assimilis*)
honeybee (*Apis mellifera*)
hooded merganser (*Lophodytes cucullatus*)
hooded warbler (*Setophaga citrina*)
horsehair worm (phylum Nematomorpha)
imperial moth (*Eacles imperialis*)
katydid (family Tettigoniidae)
largemouth bass (*Micropterus salmoides*)
loblolly pine (*Pinus taeda*)
long-jawed orb weaver (family Tetragnathidae)
longleaf pine (*Pinus palustris*)
marbled orb weaver (*Araneus marmoreus*)
mistletoe (family Loranthaceae)
mockernut hickory (*Carya tomentosa*)
mourning dove (*Zenaida macroura*)
nine-banded armadillo (*Dasypus novemcinctus*)
northern parula (*Setophaga americana*)
oldfield mouse (*Peromyscus polionotus*)
opossum (*Didelphis virginia*)
orange flea beetle (*Disonycha glabrata*)
Palamedes swallowtail (*Papilio palamedes*)
persimmon (*Diospyros virginiana*)
phantom crane fly (family Ptychopteridae)
piedmont azalea (*Rhododendron canescens*)
pileated woodpecker (*Hylatomus pileatus*)

pipevine swallowtail (*Battus philenor*)
pipsissewa (*Chimaphila maculata*)
pirate perch (*Aphredoderus sayanus*)
prothonotary warbler (*Protonotaria citrea*)
purseweb spider (*Sphodros* sp.)
raccoon (*Procyon lotor*)
red bay (*Persea palustris*)
red maple (*Acer rubrum*)
red paper wasp (*Polistes carolina*)
red-shouldered hawk (*Buteo lineatus*)
regal jumping spider (*Phidippus regius*)
river cane (*Arundinaria gigantea*)
river otter (*Lontra canadensis*)
rosy maple moth (*Dryocampa rubicunda*)
royal fern (*Osmunda spectabalis*)
rusty spider wasp (*Tachypompilus ferrugineus*)
scarlet oak (*Quercus coccinea*)
shortleaf pine (*Pinus echinata*)
southern flying squirrel (*Glaucomys volans*)
southern red oak (*Quercus falcata*)
sparkleberry (*Vaccinium arboreum*)
sphagnum moss (*Sphagnum palustre* and *S. recurvum*)
sphagnum sprite (*Nehalennia gracilis*)
spotted wintergreen (*Chimaphila maculata*)
spring treetop flasher (*Pyractomena borealis*)
stag beetle (*Lucanus capreolus*)
stonefly (order Plecoptera)
striped skunk (*Mephitis mephitis*)
striped wintergreen (*Chimaphila maculata*)
swamp sparrow (*Melospiza georgiana*)
sweet bay magnolia (*Magnolia virginiana*)
sweetgum (*Liquidambar styraciflua*)
switch cane (*Arundinaria gigantea.*)
thread-legged bug (family Reduviidae; subfamily Emesinae)
tiger beetle (*Megacephala carolina*)
trap door spider (*Ummidia* sp.)
tree cricket (family Gryllidae; subfamily Oecanthinae)
tulip poplar (*Liriodendron tulipifera*)

tupelo gum (*Nyssa aquatica*)
turbulent phosphila moth (*Phosphila turbulenta*)
turkey tail mushroom (*Trametes versicolor*)
turkey vulture (*Cathartes aura*)
turtlehead (*Chelone glabra*)
variable dancer (*Argia fumipennis*)
Virginia creeper (*Parthenocissus quinquefolia*)
Virginia snakeroot (*Aristolochia serpentaria*)
water oak (*Quercus nigra*)
white-eyed vireo (*Vireo griseus*)
white oak (*Quercus alba*)
white-tailed deer (*Odocoileus virginianus*)
wild turkey (*Meleagris gallopavo*)
wolf spider (family Lycosidae)
wood duck (*Aix sponsa*)
wood ear jelly fungus (*Auricularia auricula-judae*)
woodrat (*Neotoma floridana*)
yellow-billed cuckoo (*Coccyzus americanus*)
yellow-breasted chat (*Icteria virens*)
yellow fairy cup (*Bisporella citrina*)
yellow garden spider (*Argiope aurantia*)

Rules for Safety and Environmental Ethics

THE FOLLOWING RULES REPRESENT MY AMALGAM OF SUGGESTIONS FROM environmental educators John Byrd and Tess Moody. They conduct field trips for children and adults who have varying degrees of experience. The rules are applicable to any field trip, especially ones where reptiles and amphibians are target species. Anyone who wants to invite people for field trips to a wildlife habitat should consider giving visitors such a list, modified as necessary. Various environmental organizations have compiled similar lists tailored to fit their needs.

Never handle venomous snakes.

Do not try to guess what kind of snake it is. If you can't positively ID the snake, don't touch it.

Do not remove plants or animals from property, public or private, without express permission from the group leader or property owner.

When feasible, take photographs of wildlife in situ without handling animals or removing plants.

Any animal taken away from the capture site for photographs or examination should be released as soon as possible back at its original location.

When opportunities arise, observe animal behavior without disturbing the scene. Some interactions, such as insects pollinating plants, are common—and fascinating to watch.

Return flipped logs, rocks, organic material, and coverboards to their original positions. Leave it the way you found it.

Do not pull bark from trees or stumps or engage in any other habitat destruction.

Do not cause an animal harm in order to capture it (e.g., breaking a lizard's tail). The animal's well-being comes before human curiosity.

Do not revisit a place to which you were invited without explicit permission from the landowners or property managers.

Do not open bird boxes during bird nesting season without permission from your host.

Keep a record of your wildlife observations and a list of species encountered. If your host is keeping an inventory, offer to share your notes.

Send your host photographs of field trip participants and notable habitats, plants, animals, or fungi you observed.

Some amphibians dry out if handled. Wet your hands to protect the animals.

Do not handle any amphibian or reptile if you have bug repellent on your skin (especially hands, arms, and face). Bug repellent can kill amphibians. If feasible, limit the use of bug repellent to permethrin-treated clothing.

The US Fish and Wildlife Service recommends sanitizing field equipment. The agency also recommends not releasing animals kept in captivity into natural habitats where pathogens detrimental to amphibians may have been introduced. For example, chytrid fungus causes chytridiomycosis, an infectious disease found in US amphibian populations and in many other countries.

Index